TUTANKHAMUN
AND THE
PUZZLES
OF ANCIENT EGYPT

TUTANKHAMUN
AND THE
PUZZLES
OF ANCIENT EGYPT

DR GARETH MOORE

This edition published in 2021 by Arcturus Publishing Limited
26/27 Bickels Yard, 151–153 Bermondsey Street,
London SE1 3HA

AD008695NT

Printed in the UK

INTRODUCTION

Dear Reader,

Since my discovery of the tomb of the boy king Tutankhamun in 1922, there has been a rather dramatic surge of interest in all things concerning ancient Egypt. For me, of course, it has been a lifelong passion, but I sympathize with the newfound fascination of the general public with the treasures of this ancient civilization. I shall never forget the wonder of realizing we had finally uncovered the resting place of this legendary monarch, glittering in the candlelight, hidden for millennia.

I understand that people take a rather special interest in Tutankhamun's gilded burial mask, although there were some 5,000 other items within that would no doubt pique the interest of even the most amateur excavator. Although I am an archaeologist, I am in no way a collector of these wondrous items. Far from it, in fact—I see it as my duty to pass on these priceless artefacts to the museums and official guardians of antiquity, that they might be protected and preserved for the centuries to come.

It seems, however, that I have collected a rather large number of stories, puzzles, and riddles—and the occasional tall tale—from my extensive career in the Egyptian digs. Accordingly, the enigmas you will encounter on the following pages form something of a memoir—a personal collection of conundrums both age-old and modern that have perplexed and delighted me over the course of my employment. There are strange encryptions to decipher from the walls of long-silent tombs, tales to be pieced together from fragments of exquisitely delicate papyrus, riddles from ancient philosophers, and tests and tricks from gods and kings. There are even "brain-teasers" from my own team of excavators, who delight in the occasional battle of wits to pass the time in the midday sun.

To solve these puzzles, you will need only a sharp mind (and a sharp pencil if, like me, you are a copious note-taker). Logical deduction will be the key to unlocking most of these mysteries, for there are no trick questions. However cunningly they might have been presented to me in the first place, every puzzle has a fair and rational solution. Some of the riddles—and especially the ones related by the more frivolous members of my excavation team—involve a smattering of wordplay; if the answer seems impossible to find, you may wish to move away from the literal facts and think a little more in the abstract.

There is no need for specialist knowledge of any kind. Although a certain fondness for the facts of ancient Egypt is, naturally, encouraged, it is never required. There will be the occasional burst of mathematics, although I can assure you that you won't need a mechanical calculator to assist you—and indeed, the ancient Egyptians certainly would not have had one.

In the interest of fairness—and perhaps education—I have included solutions to all of these riddles at the back of this volume. Some of them are written down plainly, exactly as they were told to me, while others will divulge a deeper exploration of how I managed to solve a puzzle myself, for I pride myself on being methodical. In fact, if at some point you find yourself at something of an impasse in your puzzling, perhaps you might hand the solution pages over to a trusted friend or colleague, that they might formulate a hint for you and steer you towards the intended solution for any particularly tricky riddle.

I might add that, even though history and time gallop forward in their eternal linear march, you need not do the same with this book. That is to say, you may approach the puzzles in any order you like; the mysteries of the ancient world will be no less astonishing to behold, whichever way you encounter them as you journey your way through this tome.

I wish you as much success with solving these puzzles as I have had in my illustrious career, and trust that you will find your own discoveries to be equally as enlightening.

With regards,
Howard Carter, 1932

THE CODE

I remember one particular excavation several years ago, which was both fascinating and terrifying all at once. We had discovered a tomb made up of several interconnecting chambers, and yet each day another seemed to be found, revealing a sprawling complex of considerable size.

After many days of exploration, we discovered a door with what seemed to be a locking mechanism with three rotating parts, each part decorated with a variety of symbols. On the mechanism we found drawings of a cat, an egret, a bull, a jackal, a beetle, an eye and a vase.

It seemed clear that some combination and alignment of the animals would release the lock, which would allow us access to the mysterious room beyond without having to destroy any of the ancient remains.

Nearby we uncovered a series of clues, and after time spent with my hieroglyphics books decoding them we felt sure that the directions could be interpreted as follows:

Two images are correct, but only one is in the right place

The egret is correct, but is one place to the left of its correct position

Only one image is correct, but is one place to the right of its correct position

Using this information, what series of images—and in what order—did we deduce might open the lock?

THE PARTY

Archaeological expeditions are expensive pursuits, so the only way we can afford to undertake the discovery of the hidden wonders of the ancient world is through the financial support of the aristocracy.

As such, it is not an uncommon sight to behold richly dressed British peers with an interest in the pharaohs and queens of centuries past wandering the sandy paths of excavation sites. Lord Carnarvon in particular has become a great investor in my work, and I have become socially acquainted with his daughter. While wandering around the site one morning, she began to recount a story of one of the parties at Highclere Castle that she had attended recently.

> *"There were twenty-five other guests there, and Mama had kindly given me a list of all of their names to jog my memory, as I am inclined to forget these things. But once I arrived, I realized that, even with the list, I had not the slightest idea how any of the names on the list connected to the faces swimming about the room. So, at the start of the party, I decided to take my chances and randomly*

choose a name for each person, using the names from the list, which unhelpfully were all different. I was confident of my plan, and decided to stick to each allocated name for the whole evening."

My strategy did not start very well, as the first person I spoke to became most indignant when he realized I had got his name wrong. But I was not too disheartened, as I figured there must be a chance of getting some right."

I smiled at the boldness of her strategy, but then the lady asked me a question:

"After this first unfortunate encounter, what do you think the probability would have been that I had got the name of every other guest correct?"

I struggled to answer. Can you help to solve this?

THE SIBLINGS

The ineffable feeling of awe upon being first to enter a tomb that has otherwise remained unseen by human eyes for millennia is truly special. And yet it is not the glint of gold and jewels that draws me, but rather the remarkable decoration so often found in these ancient resting places. Since childhood I have been much taken by art, and the vibrant and gilded cartouches of the tomb walls fascinate me beyond description.

While poring over some sketches of decorations found during a recent excavation, I came across a series of cartouches detailing the ages and relationships of a particular family, who were an elite and powerful group from the ancient city of Thebes. The intricate inscriptions referred to five siblings: Ahmose, Beket, Hor, Khamudi and Menna.

I meticulously decoded the symbols and yet, once I had finished my task, the results were almost equally as enigmatic. The illustrations made clear that Ahmose was younger than Beket, but older than Hor. Khamudi was older than Menna, who was in turn older than Ahmose. Beket was older than Khamudi.

A final set of cartouches referred to a middle sibling—but who was this?

THE ORACLE

One of the more unsettling ancient Egyptian gods, in my opinion, is the goddess Wadjet. The protector of lower Egypt, she is depicted with the body of a woman and the head of a cobra. Despite her disconcerting appearance, this goddess was worshipped in many different ways. An oracle in her temple at Per-Wadjet provided a source of wisdom for those who sought the advice of the gods.

I once read an account of one who had visited this oracle, a great ruler hoping to resolve a conflict. He had hoped for a clear message, but all the oracle had said was that he could find value by looking at the problem from the opposite direction.

As I worked at my desk one afternoon, methodically recording the details of a selection of votive offerings to the goddess, I realized that this cryptic advice could also be applied in the modern world.

There is a number, under 100, which increases by one fifth of its value when its digits are viewed from the opposite direction—that is, when they are reversed. What is this number?

THE AMULETS

Studying the wonderfully intricate paintings on the walls of the most opulent tombs in the Valley of the Kings has the tendency to take my mind to strange places, particularly after I have resigned myself to the clutches of sleep.

Last night, I dreamed I was in the company of three gods. The dream was particularly vivid, and I noted that they were Bastet, the cat-goddess; Khepri, the scarab-god; and Sobek, the crocodile-god. They were deep in conversation, and seemed not to have registered my presence in the dream realm.

The three figures each wore a different type of amulet around their neck, with one shaped like a scarab beetle, one like a cat, and the last like a crocodile—and yet curiously no god was wearing the amulet shaped like the animal which it itself embodied. This thought had barely entered my sleeping head when I heard the gods' conversation turn to this exact subject.

"Our amulets connect us to each other this day, for none of us wears an amulet matching the animal we represent," Bastet commented in a low, silky voice.

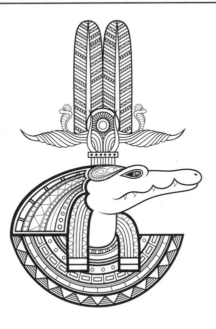

"A strange coincidence indeed," replied the god with the crocodile amulet.

When I awoke, I felt the details of my dream slowly drifting from me, and yet the words of the two gods who had spoken remained firm in my mind. The detail of which amulet had been worn by which god evaded me, however.

After I had lain in bed for a further few minutes, it came to me that it was perfectly possible to work out this information from the detail I *did* still remember.

Which god had been wearing each amulet?

THE LOCKED TOMB

With so many priceless artefacts about, it is no wonder that theft is often a problem in the Valley of the Kings. As a result, I make sure to get to know everyone who works on the sites as well as possible, removing anyone who seems untrustworthy at the first opportunity. Despite this, humans are surprising creatures, and occasionally someone who seemed honest can stray when presented with the lure of ancient gold.

After being let down by one such individual, I resolved to be more careful in my methods, trusting no one to go into the tombs alone. There was in particular one specific vault which contained treasure beyond the wildest dreams of the richest peer in Britain. To keep it safe, I contacted a purveyor of strong padlocks, who assured me that he could provide me with as many locks as I needed to secure the door.

There came a point when I needed to grant access to this secured tomb to three

archaeologists who had recently joined my team. I was adamant that none of them should enter the tomb alone, although I was comfortable with two entering together. To enforce this via the locking system, how many padlocks and keys would I need to keep the tomb secure under these rules?

What is the minimum number of padlocks and keys needed in order to ensure that all three archaeologists could enter the tomb in pairs, but none could do so alone? And how should I distribute those keys?

THE REFRESHMENT TENT

During evenings after long days spent on excavations, my team and I have taken to sharing our knowledge of ancient customs—and occasionally presenting one another with trials and challenges of our own invention.

Just yesterday evening, an amusing young man from Luxor presented a puzzle to us. He brought us nine cups, and placed them in front of us along with a jug of water. He proceeded to arrange the cups in a row, then filled the first four cups on the left of the row with water. The other five remained empty.

"Now," he said, "I challenge you to change these cups so that the order alternates between empty and filled, working along the row. But—and here is the problem—you may only touch two cups, and cannot use the jug."

At first I thought it was impossible, but then I realized how it could be done. How should this be achieved?

THE FADED SCROLL

Many artefacts found during our excavations of the ancient world have barely survived to the present day. Some tombs yield little more than scraps and fragments for archaeologists to piece together.

One such item, part of a papyrus scroll, seemed to be an account of the members of an esteemed family, with details of the names and numbers of children. Though the names remained elusive to me, and indeed to my colleagues with more experience of working with such manuscripts, one fact seemed clear—the family member described at the end of the fragment had two children, at least one of whom was a boy.

I began wondering about this ancient family, whose world must have been in many respects so very different to my own. So much in ancient times was dictated by gender—even more so than today—and so I thought further about those ancient children whose identity remained clouded in mystery. Had they both been boys?

What is the mathematical probability that both children were boys, given what we already know?

SENET SERIES

I have always found the game of Senet fascinating. The exact rules have been lost in the depths of history, yet perhaps it is this very ambiguity which piques my interest, as modern players are forced to bring their own creativity to the neat rows of squares on the board.

To my delight, my interest is shared by several of my compatriots on the excavation site, and we have collaborated to produce our own version of the Senet board. We have whiled away many a dusty evening playing together, inventing alternative versions of the game to experiment with.

Last week, a fellow archaeologist and I spent an entire evening playing Senet, and a situation arose which on reflection I realized might lead to a somewhat perplexing challenge.

I later described it to another colleague, and he indeed found it confusing. I told this colleague that after the archaeologist and I had finished our evening of Senet, we had each played five games and yet both won three of them. There were no draws.

How can this be true?

THE EXCAVATORS

I recall one particularly hot day in the Valley of the Kings, where the sun poured down on my hard-working team with all the subtlety of hailstones. I was taking some time to walk around the site, examining the progress we were making and trying to lift spirits.

During this perambulation, I overheard a conversation between two of the workers who I knew to be siblings, a brother and sister, who seemed to be discussing their family.

I listened to the sister say that she had the same number of brothers as sisters, to which the brother replied that he had double the number of sisters as brothers.

I caught the gaze of another worker nearby, and we both smiled as we realized we shared identically bewildered expressions. It was only later on while reclining in the cool of my tent that the answer came to me.

How many siblings were there in total, in the family of the brother and sister I overheard?

EVENING
ENTERTAINMENT

In the world of archaeology, one often spends extended periods of time in the company of a small group. A shared interest in the treasures of ancient Egypt and long hours of exploring sites together inevitably create a sense of camaraderie even among the most jaded of us. Indeed, however much one enjoys one's line of work, it is necessary to take an occasional break and relieve one's mind with activities unrelated to day-to-day work.

Card games have become one such pursuit that my colleagues and I have begun to indulge in of an evening. We will gather in the abode of one team member or another, or even a tent on one of the sites themselves, pour ourselves a drink, and put our minds to bridge, whist, or gin rummy.

One evening, there were four of us at the card table. An acquaintance called Jan had the responsibility of dealing, and had begun to pass out the cards in his

usual methodical manner, starting to the left of himself and working around the table in a clockwise direction. Our game required that the whole deck be dealt out.

Jan had not yet dealt half of the cards when a loud voice from outside called his name, drawing him away. He absent-mindedly took the undealt cards with him, and remained away for several minutes. The remaining players passed the time by talking among ourselves and refreshing our drinks. As a result, when our dealer returned, none of us could remember with any certainty who had received the last card that he had dealt.

Of course, we were serious players, and etiquette demanded that we shouldn't touch our half-dealt hands until all the cards in the deck were dealt—which meant that we couldn't simply count them and see which players had how many cards. Thankfully, one of our number came up with a handy solution that ensured that each person received the card they would have received had the dealing not been interrupted.

How could this be achieved?

THE QUESTION

Exploring the mystical lands of ancient Egypt, and learning more about the multitudinous gods which populated the consciousness of its inhabitants, can lead to a slumber disturbed by strange visions. Many of the nights I spent in the Valley of the Kings were filled with dreams of cats regarding me calmly with cold, golden eyes, or of tall goddesses speaking to me in languages beyond my ken.

One such night, it seemed I had slept for no more than a few seconds when I was beset with visions of a winding path, lined with vast statues. All of the statues bore the same inscription, which told me that I was in a land where all the inhabitants either always lied or always told the truth. And, more menacingly, they also told me that if my path was blocked, I must successfully identify the liars and the truth-tellers in order to be allowed to continue on my way.

Just as I was pondering how this could be done, three shadowy women stepped out from behind one of the statues, stopping me in my tracks. The first was clad in pure gold, the second in silver, and the third was dressed in green.

The gold figure stated, "Either one or both of these statements is true: the green figure is a liar; I am a truth-teller."

The silver figure then said, "It's possible that the gold figure could call me a liar."

And finally the green figure added, "Neither the gold nor silver figures are telling the truth."

I knew not where I journeyed to, but I felt certain I must pass them. I remembered the statues' inscriptions, and knew that I must identify each of them as either a liar or a truth-teller.

Can you correctly label each figure as either a liar or a truth-teller?

COIN CLASSIFICATION

Every artefact discovered in an excavation deserves equal care and attention in the classification process. In fact, I find the logging process to be extremely meditative—bringing order to the chaotic jumble deposited by the tides of history is deeply satisfying. Nowadays my colleagues do much of the logging for me, but I still choose to keep my hand in when the mood takes me.

I remember one recent evening spent working through a collection of coins which we had unearthed near Karnak. I examined each one in turn, recording the details of each tiny disc, but started to feel my eyes growing weary as I neared the end of my task. I was anxious not to miss any details, so in order to give my mind a break I decided to consider the coins in a different way.

I laid twelve of the coins on the table in front of me and observed the random patterns they seemed to form in relation to one another. I absent-mindedly moved them around—but then, while I was moving them, I realized that I could arrange the twelve coins into six straight lines, each made up of four coins.

How could I achieve these six lines of four coins, using the twelve coins I had?

SCHEDULING THE DIG

In the world of archaeology, the spectacular finds are few and far between—and yet it is the thought of wonderous discoveries that motivates us to come back day after day to the ancient ruins of Egypt. I often take responsibility for assigning duties, dividing up the sites we work on into sections which will be tackled by different members of my team.

I have learned gradually over the years how long it takes the average archaeologist to cover particular areas, and those I work with are now mercifully more or less as fast as each other. We divide the site into equally sized blocks, sized such that four archaeologists can excavate four blocks in four days.

I recently received a letter from Lord Carnarvon, informing me that his patience in funding my recent excavations was wearing thin due to the lack of high-profile discoveries, and that the money might soon be withdrawn. However, I felt certain that we could make a breakthrough if we could only get through the next thirty blocks, so I wrote back to Lord Carnarvon to ask for twenty days to prove myself.

How many archaeologists would I need to excavate the thirty blocks in twenty days, assuming they worked at a constant rate?

ENTERING THE
TOMB

The tombs of ancient Egypt are prone to surprising many who enter with their vast complexes of passageways and chambers. As soon as one thinks the excavation is complete, new openings are liable to appear, presenting all the more mystery—and often even more ancient artefacts.

I remember clearly one such tomb, which I had explored with a team of three others, named Mace, Lythgoe, and Burton. We had spent some time progressing carefully through a long passageway, when we came to a curious and extremely steep section of tunnelling which was too narrow to be traversed by more than two people at once. As by this point we only had one lantern, following a rather unfortunate accident, it was necessary to come up with a system whereby our source of illumination could be transported back and forth. This would involve one of us carrying it back to those left behind at each stage.

All of us practised somewhat different levels of caution when climbing in these situations, with some

members of our party
moving more slowly than
others. After some brief
discussion, we established
that Mace would take
five minutes to traverse
the tunnel, Lythgoe
would take ten minutes,
and Burton would take
twenty minutes. Being of
a cautious disposition, I
myself would take twenty-
five minutes to pass
through.

After a brief discussion,
Lythgoe presented a
solution which allowed
us all to travel through the tunnel in a reasonably
economical length of time, and without having to
climb in the dark. At no point should anyone climb
without the lantern, so the two people climbing
up would always need to travel at the speed of the
slowest person until they had reached the other side,
whereupon one of them could then return to the
remaining party.

What was the shortest amount of time in which all
four of us could pass through the tunnel, using the
lantern to illuminate our path?

THE SCHOLAR

Scholars are a strange and varied species. I have noted over the years that some possess a great capacity for understanding the most complex corners of philosophy, and yet are utterly bewildered when it comes to simple matters of common sense. Others have the most peculiar methods of recalling information, with the logical ordering that may seem intuitive to an outsider seemingly making no sense to them at all.

I knew one such individual several years ago, and one incident in particular springs to mind. He had been analyzing a particularly beautiful specimen of artwork from the Old Kingdom period, a depiction of five kings: Sneferu, Khafre, Menkaure, Khufu, and Djedefre. My knowledge of history for this period was not strong, and during the course of our conversation I asked him in which order these great monarchs had taken to the throne.

He thought for some time, but could only come up with the following facts:

- Khafre became pharaoh later than Djedefre

- Djedefre became pharaoh later than Khufu

- Menkaure became pharaoh later than Sneferu

- Sneferu became pharaoh earlier than Khafre

- Khufu became pharaoh immediately after Sneferu

- Khufu became pharaoh earlier than Khafre

- Djedefre became pharaoh earlier than Menkaure

- Khafre became pharaoh earlier than Menkaure

Although all valid and true, this information took some time to make sense of due to its confusing nature.

What is the correct ordering of rulers, from latest to earliest?

THE GAME NIGHT

My compatriots and I had spent an evening playing cards, and toward the end of the evening had even wagered a few coins on the results.

I could see eyelids beginning to droop, and suggested that we turn in for the night. However, one of the players objected, exclaiming that he would give us a chance to win back what we had lost. Curious, I agreed. At this he produced a bag, and explained:

> *"In this bag, I have six different kinds of coin. Each kind of coin has a different monetary value, and there is an equal number of each type of coin in the bag, giving a total of forty-two coins.*

> *"I will give you the chance to draw however many coins you like. However, you must decide exactly how many coins you will draw before you take your first coin, and none may be put back into the bag once they have been removed.*

> *"I will pay you back if, after you have drawn your coins, you have in your hand at least three of each kind of coin, so long as you have not taken more coins than you needed to be sure of such a result."*

What is the exact number of coins I would have had to take out of the bag to fulfil these requirements?

THE SCRIBE'S ACCOUNT

I once studied a fascinating scroll which described two families of farmers who grew grain for bread. The artefact gave a detailed account of how many bags of grain each family member had managed to grind over a certain period.

Each of the two families was made up of a mother, father and two children—in both cases a boy and a girl. Each family had managed to grind fifty bags of grain in total, and in each family the girl had ground more bags of grain than the boy. To be specific, in one family the girl had ground one bag more than the boy, while in the other the girl had ground four bags more than the boy.

While poring over these accounts, I also noticed a strange quirk: in each family, if I squared the number of bags of grain ground individually by the mother and each child, the sum of these three squares was equal to the quantity of bags of grain ground by the father when also squared.

How many bags of grain had been ground by each family member in each family?

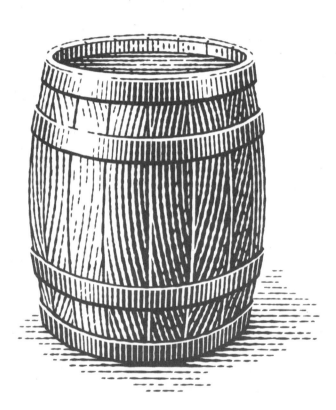

THE WATER BARREL

In the heat of the desert, drinking water is an essential commodity—even sitting in the shade often necessitates an elevated consumption.

We have a water barrel in a shady corner of the site, and I ensure that someone is appointed to see that it remains topped up, fetching water to refill as necessary. To prevent anyone going thirsty while they wait for refills to be brought, I always ask the appointed individual to fetch a refill as soon as the barrel is less than half full of water.

One afternoon, I was disturbed by the raised voice of the boy I had entrusted with collecting water for the day. He was arguing with a fellow worker, whom I had given the task to the day before.

On further investigation, the subject of their disagreement transpired to be about how full the barrel was. The youth in charge of the water today perceived the perfectly symmetrical barrel to be just under half-empty, while his colleague was adamant that the barrel was just over half-full.

Despite the clear arbitrariness of whether it was *exactly* half full or not, I was able to intervene and suggest an easy method for determining who was correct on this particular matter.

How did I work out who was right? The barrel was not labelled with a halfway line.

THE NIGHTMARE

Just a few nights ago, I was once again plunged into that strange dreamland where I had met shadowy figures before, a land which I knew to be populated with those who either always lied or always told the truth. However, in this particular dream, I found that I knew of a third state—some who I encountered on my way might also be *occasional* liars—those who sometimes told the truth, and sometimes lied.

I found myself wandering along the winding path of which I had dreamed before, peopled with tall statues,

waiting for the moment when my progress would be stopped once again. And, as expected, eventually three figures, all of varying heights, stopped me in my tracks.

The three figures held out their hands, motioning for me to be still, and presented me with three statements.

"I always tell the truth" said the tallest figure.

"The tallest man always tells the truth", said the figure of middle height.

"I sometimes lie, but sometimes tell the truth", said the smallest figure.

I realized I also knew that each was of a different type—so one was a liar, one a truth-teller, and one could do both. And I further realized that I must once against identify which of the three types each figure was, at which I found myself yanked back into consciousness by the dilemma. Yet once again, as I lay in the darkness and quiet, I discovered I had enough information to discern the nature of each of these three figures.

Which of the three figures was a liar, which was an occasional liar, and which was a truth-teller?

THE COUNTERFEIT SCARAB

During a recent conversation with a colleague, talk turned to a collection of scarab amulets which had been discovered near Luxor. We had thought that there were nine in total, but one of the specialists within the service then identified that one of the amulets was a counterfeit produced relatively recently—the composition of the faience differed from that used in the originals.

Shortly afterwards, the curator vented to me his annoyance that the specialist who had identified the counterfeit beetle had placed it back among the genuine amulets—and that as they were all essentially visually indistinguishable from each other, the curator had no reliable way of identifying the fake.

I enquired of the distressed curator as to whether he had a set of balancing scales. Upon receiving an affirmative response, I suggested he use a series of comparisons using those very scales to identify the counterfeit amulet, since the one thing we did know was that the genuine amulets all weighed the same, but that the fake one was lighter than the rest.

What would be the minimum number of comparisons to make with the balancing scales that would be *guaranteed* to work out which of the nine amulets was the fake one?

LOOKING FOR DIRECTIONS

When I first arrived in Egypt and witnessed the vast complex at Thebes, I admit I felt a tinge of uncertainty. This land was so far away, so alien from my home. My hesitation soon disappeared, however, at the first sight of great pillars engraved with hieroglyphs, and my love of the ancient world took primacy in a flash.

As in any new location, it took me a few days to become properly acquainted with the paths and passageways that led to different sites of interest. I took long walks, familiarizing myself with the locality.

On one such walk, after setting out from Karnak for the centre of Luxor, I found myself at an intersection of several paths, but the signpost had been blown over and was lying intact, covered in dust next to the junction.

On picking it up I found that Luxor and Karnak had been included among several other destinations, but unfortunately it was no longer possible to see which way it had once been pointing.

How could I ascertain which direction to continue in?

SITE DISPUTE

I like to imagine that most of the work that needs doing on the sites I supervise is reasonably interesting—but still the occasional disagreement arises, with some individuals more enthused about certain jobs than others.

One morning, I overheard two men on the site having one such argument. They had been assigned different areas to work that day, yet both were keen to work on the same patch. To resolve the dispute, I decided to set them a challenge. I had in my possession two bags of faience amulets, all of a similar shape and size, but of two different shades.

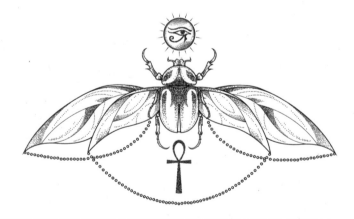

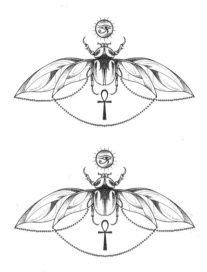

One bag contained green amulets, the other contained blue. Each bag contained ten amulets.

I presented the two bags to one of the men, and told him that he could arrange the amulets however he wished between the two bags, and that once he had finished this, I would blindly remove one amulet from a bag chosen at random. If the amulet I drew was green, he would get to work at his site of choice. If the amulet was blue, his fellow worker would get to choose.

As the man began to rearrange the amulets, it occurred to me that he could organize the amulets in such a way that he would have a distinct advantage. How could he arrange the amulets to give me the best chance of drawing him a green amulet?

THE COIN TOSS

One evening in the aftermath of the discovery of the boy king's treasures in Tutankhamun's tomb, Lord Carnarvon and I raised a glass to our success, and spent time discussing the magic of the event. Conversation also turned to the less exciting subject of a certain journalist who would shortly be arriving to speak to one of us, and for various reasons which I shall not enter into, neither of us much wished to speak to him. We eventually decided to flip a coin to decide who would be the one to meet him. I rummaged in my desk for a coin to toss, eventually finding a somewhat dusty penny.

Later on, we got to talking about the coin toss (which I won, I am glad to say). We all know that if we call heads or tails we have a one in two chance of being correct but, we pondered, how would this change if one bet instead that "heads" would appear at least once when tossing a coin twice in a row?

Carnarvon observed that there were only three outcomes that mattered: a loss, which required "tails" on both tosses; or a win, which would be either "tails" first but then "heads" on the second toss, or simply "heads" on the first toss. Therefore, he argued, the chances of winning were clearly two in three.

Is he correct?

HISTORICAL SENET

While studying an account of ancient Egyptian social life in the city of Thebes, I discovered a fascinating description of a series of Senet games which had taken place between three high-ranking officials in the city. The three officials were Khay, Thutmose and Prehotep.

They had engaged in a tournament where the winner of each game, which involved two of them playing against each other, would keep their seat at the board. The losers, meanwhile, would take it in turns to play. Competition had been stiff, and there had been twenty-one games in total. Khay had taken part in ten games, Thutmose in fourteen games and Prehotep in eighteen games.

I could also see from the historical record that Prehotep had done very well, and had played the first fifteen games before sitting out the sixteenth.

As I read on, the text began to fragment and become less clear. There seemed to be some interesting detail about the life of one of the players, but all I could work out was that the person referred to had lost the eighteenth game. After some thought, I realized that I could work out who it was from the information I had.

Which two competitors played in the eighteenth game in the tournament, and who won that game?

ANCIENT LOVERS

I have spent much time around the wonders of the ancient world—the gold caskets and chariots of kings, sarcophagi and canopic jars, and the inscriptions of gods beyond the wildest imaginings of many in the Western world. As a result, I am often called upon at events or in conversation to recount some of the myths and legends which have been gathered from the Egyptian civilizations.

Some of my favourite stories to tell are those of ancient lovers: the powerful Cleopatra and her affair with Mark Anthony; or the dedication of Isis gathering the fragments of Osiris and putting them back together, after they had been scattered across Egypt by the god Seth.

Another story I often tell is based on images found on the walls of an obscure tomb in a quiet corner of Egypt. The images tell the story of two young lovers who lived in towns on opposite banks of the Nile— two towns which had become engaged in terrible warfare. A bridge joined the towns but, as a result of the conflict, no one from either town could cross the bridge to visit the other. The bridge was the only method of getting from one town to the other, and it

was guarded by a fierce sentry who ensured that no one crossed it, day or night. It took ten minutes for someone to walk across the bridge, and the sentry sat in a small hut exactly halfway across the bridge, emerging from his lair every five minutes on the dot to check that no one was attempting the crossing.

The lovers, Sabni and Satiah, had become more and more frustrated with this situation—they could wave to each other from across the river, but nothing more. One day, Sabni decided to take matters into his own hands, and cross the bridge. He needed to make a plan, but knew that he could not cross the bridge in under five minutes even if he ran across. He also knew that although he could just about reach the guard's hut in five minutes, there was nowhere he could conceal himself in order to avoid being seen.

After some thought he devised a plan which he thought would be likely to deceive the guard. He was cheered by the thought that the guards came from a different town altogether, so he would not be recognized.

When recounting this tale, I am in the habit of asking my audience if they can guess what Sabni's plan for crossing the bridge was. What do you think the answer is?

THE TAX COLLECTORS

Some of the surviving records from ancient Egypt tell of the trading practices of the day, including about taxes and how they were levied.

One particular account stays with me, of a specific trade route in north Egypt. Those who journeyed along the route invariably carried grain, a commodity which was often bartered at the time. The route crossed five bridges, and at each bridge a collector would levy a tax on all who passed through. The sum owed was always half of all of the bags of grain that each trader who wanted to pass through was carrying, rounded down.

Along with their steep rates, however, the tax collectors had developed a system of goodwill, where after the tariff had been paid they would return one bag of grain to each trader.

Despite the goodwill, this seemed a steep tax indeed. If I had been an ancient trader, how many bags would I have needed to set out with in order to reach the end of the trade route with exactly two bags of grain to sell?

THE CATTLE COUNT

When considering ancient taxation practices, it is hard not to regret the staid nature of our own modern approach to such things. In ancient Egypt, cattle counts, which were sometimes used to calculate taxes, could be grand events full of social excitement. While considering a document detailing a cattle count from the Old Kingdom, I noticed a surprising arrangement of hieroglyphs which I knew to all represent numbers. Written in modern script, these numbers were as follows:

2, 3, 6, 7, 8, 10, 11, 12, 13, 14, 19 and 20.

I assumed them to be records of the quantity of cattle owned by particular Egyptians, perhaps within certain family groups. However, before I investigated the meaning of the numbers any further, I happened to notice that this set of twelve numbers could be split into four groups of equal size using a decidedly non-mathematical rule. I had a notebook handy and so made a quick note, fully intending to perplex Lord Carnarvon at our next meeting:

2, 6, 10

3, 7, 8

11, 12, 20

13, 14, 19

What rule had I used to sort the twelve numbers into these four groups?

THE DIFFICULT ARCHAEOLOGISTS

I have been fortunate enough in my career to work with some most pleasant people in the business of archaeology, who share my own relish for investigating the lives of the pharaohs, and who are content to work in somewhat warmer climes than Kensington. However, there are others, as in any profession I suppose, who simply cannot bring themselves to get along with anyone they take the slightest dislike to.

The most memorable (and indeed problematic) time when I met such people was when a group of five of them arrived at the site I was supervising in Deir el-Bahari. The five men, Albert, Edwin, Martin, Percy, and Arthur, had arrived from England together, but (most inconveniently) they had arrived on the wrong side of the Nile, so had to commission a small boat to carry them across. Even more inconveniently, it seemed that a strong antipathy had developed between some of the members of the party on the journey, a dislike so strong that certain pairs of them

could not stand to be alone in each other's company, not even for the length of time it took to cross the river.

Albert could not stand Edwin, Edwin could not abide Martin, Martin hated Percy, and Percy despised Arthur. Charming.

Having heard of these tensions, I was concerned that a fight might break out if any of these pairs were left to stand together on a river bank, even if others were present—for strange, aristocratic reasons, the driver of the boat was the only person they would not argue in front of. However, the boat available only had space for a maximum of two people, besides the boat driver. At first I thought that it might be necessary to find another boat, but the driver suggested a neat strategy for getting all five men across the river without risking any outbreaks of fisticuffs.

How could this be done?

THE CURSED DREAM

There are many superstitious fears which surround the tombs of the pharaohs. Indeed, some believe that opening the tombs and disturbing the treasures within will awake a terrible curse, which will hunt those who dare to venture within.

During the daylight hours I can easily dismiss these rumours as sensationalist nonsense, but I find that once the sun has set and I retire alone to my quarters, my mind is liable to twist and turn with thoughts of ancient, vengeful gods made flesh, and mummies walking the dusky passageways of their tombs.

Just last night, I dreamed that I was being pursued through a complex of corridors by a hideous, faceless figure, trailing bandages yellowed with age. I darted from room to room, searching for some method of escape. I had finally passed through a door which seemed to lead to an exit when my heart was filled with horror: I heard the door click shut behind me, a key turn in the lock, and a dreadful laugh from outside.

I soon realized that the exit I had seen was at the end of a corridor made of thick glass. The floor was

littered with insects which had been burned to a crisp
by the encasement's ability to magnify the sun's rays,
focussing it on those within. I cast my eyes around
the passage, but found the door at the other end of
the corridor to be my only possible exit. Although I
could see it led to the freedom of the outside world, I
dared not risk travelling through the glass passage for
fear of being burned myself. But was it a preferable
alternative to facing the dreadful wraith who prowled
behind the locked door I had just passed through?
Having looked through the keyhole I could see the
spirit waited patiently, like a cat stalking its prey.

I awoke in a cold sweat, the images of my
nightmare deeply imprinted on my mind. And yet, as
I lay in my bed, listening to a cool wind blow over the
Egyptian landscape, an idea came to me—a way in
which I could have potentially escaped with my life.

How could I have escaped the corridor without injury?

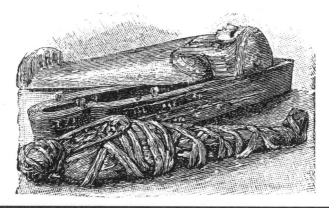

THE FLOOD

E ach year, as the monsoon season ends, huge volumes of water rush down from the highlands of Ethiopia, inundating Egypt with life-giving water.

Whenever this season comes, I am led to a memory of an elderly Egyptian I once knew, who at the time lived near the banks of the Nile. The flood was of great importance to him, and he had built a small reservoir which connected to the river through a slim channel. He had carefully measured the volume of water that the reservoir could hold and had installed a gauge to measure the water level.

He once told me that during the previous year the progression of water levels had been such that the level increased exponentially each day, with as much new water arriving on each day as had arrived in the entire season to date. On the fourteenth afternoon of that season his reservoir became entirely full, and had started to overflow.

Given it took almost fourteen days to fill, on what day had it reached just half of its capacity?

MAGICAL NUMBERS

I sometimes contemplate how modern scholars must think differently about language when compared to their ancient counterparts. The economical lines and strokes of our alphabets are so far removed from the illustrations of ancient Egypt—and what artists those long-ago scribes must have been, tracing hawks, human figures, and magical eyes.

After spending so much time gazing upon hieroglyphs, and tracing their development into more modern scripts, I have begun to look more closely at the shape of the numbers we use today. These too can be considered as images in their own right, with the swan-like elegance of the "2", or the two neatly stacked pebbles that form an "8".

During a recent conversation with Lord Carnarvon he mentioned that he had read a small item in the newspaper about a rather large number: 8,549,176,320. This number was also rather elegant, although not in a pictorial fashion.

What is pleasing about this number?

THE SECURITY GUARDS

After the discovery of the unearthly beauties of Tutankhamun's tomb, it was natural to expect a flurry of visitors, desperate to catch a glimpse of the treasures contained therein for themselves. I grew increasingly concerned about thieves, for the tomb was filled with valuable treasure and it seemed inevitable that some opportunistic felons might try their luck. As a result, we decided to appoint some trustworthy members of our team to man the entrance to the tomb.

Though a simple enough idea in theory, it proved to be something of a challenge to organize. Eventually we found four volunteers who we could trust to guard the door: Hasina, Khalid, Anthony, and Maat.

We decided that there should be two people on duty at all times, and that each of the four volunteers should work two six-hour shifts in each twenty-four hour period. So that no one got too tired, we agreed that no one should work two shifts back-to-back. Naturally, we figured that if both guards swapped places with someone else at the same time, the

security of the tomb would be compromised, so we stipulated that the timetable should only allow one swap at any one time.

However, they all had various time constraints: Hasina wanted to start at 8pm and be done by midday; Khalid said he couldn't work between 6am and midday; Anthony wanted to take over after Khalid's second shift; and Maat wanted to be working at 5am.

It took some working with many crossings-out on a piece of paper—however, we were all eventually able to come to an arrangement which worked for everyone. To make things easier, we agreed that each shift should start and end on the hour.

What hours did the four volunteers each end up spending guarding the door to the tomb?

LADY EVELYN'S NOTE

Much of my work here in Egypt would be impossible without the generous funding of Lord and Lady Carnarvon. Lord Carnarvon in particular has been completely consumed with fascination for the Egyptian world, and is gathering quite a collection of antiquities in Highclere Castle, the almost impossibly grand country estate which he and his wife call home.

The aristocratic couple's daughter has also developed quite a taste for the subject, and as such often accompanies her father on his trips. I have known her since she was a child, and we get on well enough—indeed, on her latest visit, she took to leaving me cryptic notes containing riddles and puzzles in an attempt to divert me from (as she sees it) my obsession with Egyptian history.

The latest riddle read as follows:

A progression of letters, but how do they progress? Untangle my meaning and Osiris will judge you kindly, when that time comes for your heart to be weighed and for your soul to be judged.

Tell me: what three letters are missing from this strange sequence?

T M W T L A M F _ _ _

And indeed, what three letters were missing?

THE FRAGMENTS OF PAPYRUS

Texts describing the rituals of mummification are few and far between, so I was most animated to learn of a discovery of one such papyrus at a dig not far from where I was based at the time. I eventually managed to organize a time when I could view the documents for myself.

As is often the way with ancient parchment, the artefact was delicate and was in several pieces, as a result of many centuries of age and no doubt the further disturbance of being removed from its resting place. However, the historians involved had managed to translate some of the hieroglyphs, and they seemed to form a list of objects connected with the embalming ritual, broken into several fragments. I have transcribed the list of fragments here, using English equivalents:

AMU AR BAN CAN CJ COP DA EN GE GUS HA INC LET MA OPI SAR SE SK

After some effort, we managed to decode the six objects, one of which was made up of two words rather than one.

What was the original list of objects?

A MATTER OF TIME

As the sun scorched its path through the sky this morning, I found myself sitting outside an open tomb, considering the intricacies of the passage of time—something which is rather inescapable to an archaeologist, I suppose. I cast my mind back to a strange event which had occurred last week, shortly after I had discovered, along with a fellow excavator, the remains of what seemed to be a calendar.

We were somewhat engrossed by the long-gone days and months mapped out by this obsolete almanac, and then began instead to discuss our own, and the patterns of the months and seasons with which we are most familiar. My compatriot remarked on the similarities between this Egyptian calendar and our Gregorian one, and marvelled that the habits of the timekeepers of yore meant that our calendars are both constructed of months which last such a similar length of time. The symmetry of it all is quite impressive, he said, considering how many of our own months have thirty days, just as the Egyptian calendar did.

I refuted this claim, as a matter of principle—in fact, only one third of our modern months have thirty days, so the striking similarity is only *one third* as striking. My colleague, however, was not satisfied with my denial—in fact, he stated that my calculation was quite incorrect.

I insisted that exactly four of our modern months consist of thirty days, and he insisted again that I was wrong. I asked him, in the politest but surest terms, to illustrate exactly how many months he felt must satisfy the calculation, according to his thinking.

What do you think he said?

VISION

I profoundly dislike those archaeologists who boast loudly of their findings. As you know, I loathe to be thought of as a "treasure hunter", blithely ignorant of the historical significance of our work and instead searching only for trinkets and shiny objects. But there is one such excavator—whose name I shall not reveal, in the interests of professionalism—who has developed a most unique style of bragging, which I cannot bear. His finds are always the biggest, the most unlikely, the most sought-after; you would think he uncovered the secrets of the very universe with every dig he conducted—while in contrast I often find his unearthed pieces to be rather mundane.

I had the misfortune of being joined by this gentleman recently at a dinner, and with him intending, I presume, to belittle my discoveries and shamelessly trumpet his own, he started up a conversation about his latest project. The term "conversation" here is used rather loosely, and "monologue" might be more accurate, but I digress.

He began to tell me that he had just last week been excavating an ancient temple and, to his joy and delight, had discovered a most antiquated marvel

encased within the walls of its inner shrine. It was, he said, an amazing invention which had allowed the ancient architects and inhabitants of the temple to see through the walls.

> *"Imagine that!" said he, his eyes full of misplaced rapture, "The ingenuity of this civilization is quite astonishing to me. We have much to learn, do we not, we humble diggers?"*

I merely rolled my eyes at this; "humble" was not the striking characteristic of this fellow diner. I couldn't think of anything kind to say about his discovery, so I didn't say anything at all. After all, I knew exactly what kind of object he was describing, and I would not personally have been so silly as to classify it as an extraordinary invention.

What do you think he had found, in the walls of the shrine?

MISCHIEVOUS TWINS

On one dig I presided over, I clearly remember a day where I came across a set of twins from Cairo, both of whom possessed a wide, mischievous grin and walked with a spring in their step. On enquiring as to their names from one of my colleagues on the dig, I discovered that they were known as Ammon and Baahir.

During this conversation, I also gleaned that the twins had become somewhat unpopular among those who knew them, as they had decided that for the whole of that week they would either tell the truth at all times, or lie at every opportunity. They had not made clear which of them would take which path, or indeed if they would both lie or both tell the truth.

The next time I saw the two twins together that week, I spontaneously approached them, asking without much forward planning who was the lying twin and who was the truth-teller.

Ammon pointed at Baahir, and declared that "he is the liar". Directly afterwards, Baahir replied that "neither of us are liars".

This perplexed me a little at first, and I began to regret my haste in asking my question. Yet after some consideration, I worked out that I could discern which of the twins were liars (if any) and which truth-tellers (if any).

Can you identify the rule each twin was using—was each telling the truth or lying?

HIEROGLYPH
FASCINATION

I am captivated by the *Book of the Dead*, the magical collection of spells and incantations which instructed those who dwelled in the ancient world as to how their bodies could progress from the fleeting world of the living to the sacred halls of the dead. What comfort it must have been to ancient kings, to know that their spiritual journey would be one guided by the advice of their wisest counsellors.

Yet the *Book of the Dead* is just one of such texts, and other such funerary inscriptions can be found in the ancient cities of Egypt, if one looks closely. I was particularly intrigued by a set of spells which I found delicately painted onto a shroud, found deep within a tomb complex in the Valley of the Kings. As I scanned the lines of the hieroglyphs, grown faint with age, an interesting thought struck me about the systems of our own writing. I quickly got out my notebook, and jotted down some letters:

A, E, F, H, I, K, L, M, N, T, V, W, X, Y, Z

C, J, O, S, U

B, D, G, P, R

I fully intended to enclose these lists in my next correspondence with Lord Carnarvon, knowing how frustrated he can get at puzzles which are not immediately obvious to him.

What rule had I used to group the letters into three sets? And why might I have omitted "Q"?

A NEW JUG

At a market stall I became enraptured with a small jug, due to its design of hieroglyphs surrounding the ever-haunting eye of Horus. However, in my foolishly hasty preparation of a cup of much-needed tea one morning, I knocked the jug off the table whereupon it shattered on the floor, beyond all repair.

I was keen to replace it, and returned at the first opportunity to the same market stall, but found to my surprise that the stall now sold small bunches of flowers. I nearly gave up entirely, but then noticed that the flowers were sold in the same small jugs that I sought, with each bunch in a jug costing the equivalent of £16, for both the flowers and the jug. I had no need for flowers, so asked the stall-keeper how much it would be for the jug alone—she (somewhat enigmatically) replied that the flowers were worth £10 more than the jug.

According to the stall-holder, therefore, how much was the jug worth by itself?

ANOTHER NOTE FROM EVELYN

I sometimes fear that my preoccupation with the long-since dead and buried makes me something of a bore to those who find excitement in this century. However, along with the patronage and support of the Carnarvon family I also from time to time enjoy the benefits of their social connections.

Lady Evelyn, the daughter of the esteemed Lord Carnarvon has, as I have mentioned, taken to taxing my mind with various brain teasers. I am occasionally annoyed by her deliberate attempts to divert me from my work, but one note she sent me recently caught my attention sufficiently to draw me away from the selection of canopic jars I was then preoccupied with.

It read as follows:

I am thinking of an increasing adjectival sequence that begins: Nation, Timing, Pronged, Poster

Which of these could come next in the sequence: Violin, Night, Star, or Cave?

What was the solution to her riddle?

THE MARKET TRADER

The Nile, with its sprawling delta, winding path and lurking crocodiles, is the beating heart of Egypt. There are many legends surrounding its waters, and most of the activity in the country centres on its ebb and flow.

While visiting Cairo, I got talking to a tradesman who owned a market stall, and discovered that he had to cross the river by boat each day in order to transport his goods from his hometown to the market. It sounded a difficult commute, especially when I took a closer look at his stall and saw he traded in both livestock and bags of animal food. It was nearing the end of the day, and he was packing up his stall with just a goat, a duck and a bag of duck food left.

When I expressed my thoughts to him, the trader commented that it was indeed a tricky journey, since his boat was so small that he could only take one of those three things with him at a time—which I felt was rather impractical in this man's line of trade, but that's by the by. Secondly, the animals were rather

spirited in nature. If left together without the trader, the goat would chase away the duck and, similarly, if the duck was left alone with the duck food, the food would get eaten. Wanting to keep both of his animals and the food, the market trader had come up with a method of crossing the river, given that thankfully each of his animals was happy being left alone on the bank, and wouldn't run away.

How did the trader get both of his animals and the bag of food across the Nile?

THE ARCHITECTS

The tales of ancient Egypt often jump swiftly between the realms of gods and mortals. Immortal beings with the heads of animals can wander into the lives of humans at will, causing whatever joy or terror they please.

I heard one such story from an old woman in Luxor, who ran a restaurant I frequented from time to time. It was a tale of three Egyptian architects who had lived in the period of the Middle Kingdom, all extremely advanced in their field, who had entered into competition with each other over the latest palace desired by the pharaoh. They had each pitched their plan to the great advisors of the kingdom, and had been deemed to be equally brilliant in their thoughts and designs. As a result, the advisors had decided to set them a challenge to determine who would get to design the palace.

They summoned the three architects to their chambers

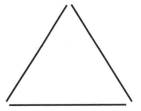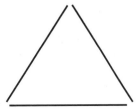

and, once they were all assembled, gave them their task. They took six short reeds from a small box, and arranged them into two triangles on the table in front of the architects:

> "The winner will be the first to successfully come up with a method for rearranging these reeds to form four triangles, so that all four of those triangles are equal in size. The ends of the reeds can touch each other, but no other parts of a reed may be touching in your solution."

The three competing architects sat still, deep in contemplation of the puzzle. Eventually one of them gave a solution.

How did the architect propose to successfully rearrange the reeds? The solution did not involve breaking any of the reeds into smaller pieces.

DINNER WITH CARNARVON

On one of Carnarvon's visits to Luxor, I hosted him for dinner at my residence. But, just as we began to eat, all electrical power to the building was lost and we were plunged into total darkness.

This was of no great consequence as I had ample stock of candles in the house, as well as a ready supply of matches with which to light them. However, while we were in the dark, I saw an opportunity to present my sponsor with a small intellectual challenge:

> *"On the table in front of you is a small basket containing four bread rolls. Two are white, and two are brown. While we are waiting for the candles to be lit, how could you distribute all of the rolls between us without looking at them, so that we both end up with identical amounts of both white and brown bread on our plates? I note also that both types of bread weigh and feel the same, and that eating some or all of the bread, or not placing some or all of it onto our plates, would be considered cheating."*

Carnarvon was silent for a second while he thought, but when light was restored I saw that he had successfully completed my challenge.

How did he do it?

THE DIFFICULT JOURNEY

Lord Carnarvon had faced a challenging journey from Cairo on his latest visit to the Valley of the Kings. He had planned to take a boat down the Nile, but when it reached the town of Naqadah it had broken down and he had been forced to disembark and seek other methods of transport.

First, he managed to beg a lift from a motorcar driver. Throughout the journey, the car went eight times as fast as he could have progressed on foot, and it took him half of the way from Naqadah to the Valley of the Kings. At this point, the driver had reached his own destination, and did not drive any further.

For the rest of the journey, Carnarvon was forced to travel on a cart drawn by donkeys, which was slowed by a heavy load. While he sat, he worked out that he could have walked at double the speed of the cart.

Would Carnarvon have saved time on this exhausting journey by walking all the way from Naqadah, assuming that he would have had enough energy to walk at the same speed for the whole journey without stopping?

DAILY DISTRACTION

When I have the time, I enjoy the categorizing of ancient artefacts. Examining each item and ascertaining its original use can be deeply satisfying.

However, this satisfaction can give rise to less desirable consequences. I recently felt so consumed by a classification project that I became lost in myself, oblivious to the passing of time. I spent many hours at my desk, speaking with no one, completely absorbed by the wild eyes of the gods and pharaohs before me.

When I eventually emerged from this reverie, I felt confused, unclear as to how long I had spent on my task, indeed as to whether it had been hours or days. I walked out into the blinding sun, refamiliarizing myself with the human world. "What day is it?", I asked one of my close colleagues who happened to be passing, half in jest, and yet half quite serious.

His reply was, to say the least, somewhat cryptic:

"At the time when the day before yesterday was tomorrow, it was two days after Friday."

What day of the week was it when I asked my question?

A GAME OF
HANDBALL

The long days of digging, chipping away at areas without the certainty of finding anything of interest, can be gruelling for those who work on excavations. I vividly remember one such period before the great discovery of Tutankhamun's tomb, filled with endless days of drudgery and disappointment, when my workers were rewarded with nothing but piles of dust. Funding was dwindling, and it seemed as if we may have had to abandon our efforts entirely, consigning our work to the great scrapheap of archaeological attempts.

On occasion, after such days of fruitless toiling, the workers indulged in certain games as the evening cooled. I wonder at the parallels with the ancient world, as to whether the inhabitants of the New Kingdom also threw balls to one another, laughing in the golden glow of an Egyptian sunset.

I remember engaging in conversation one morning with one of the men who worked on the site, a young fellow by the name of Gamal, who had a cheeky manner. The previous evening he had been involved in

a game of handball—an event which I myself had not witnessed, having been too absorbed in my work. He recounted some of the particulars of the game to me, but in my sleep-deprived state—and having not been at the event myself—I did not fully follow his blow-by-blow account, with my thoughts wandering back to a particularly fine collection of scarabs I had been classifying. However, my attention was caught by a sentence which struck me as somewhat odd:

> *"I had just walked off the field when I happened to look to my left, and saw my friend Hasani about fifty yards away. I changed direction and walked towards him. Yet after I had walked fifty yards towards him, and he had walked fifty yards too—with us both facing each other the whole time—we were still fifty yards apart!"*

How could this have been the case?

A LUNCH
APPOINTMENT

I once journeyed to Cairo in order to keep an appointment for lunch with an esteemed colleague from the Egyptian Antiquities Service—a man extremely advanced in his field, who had made many inspired archaeological decisions and had been rewarded with some breathtaking finds.

After we had partaken of a most satisfactory meal, we retired to a quiet corner to drink coffee and discuss our latest breakthroughs in the investigation of the ancient world.

As we spoke, I learned that my compatriot's excavations had led him to four particular discoveries: a set of golden amulets; a collection of intricately painted earthenware pots; a sarcophagus from the Middle Kingdom; and a set of richly decorated canopic jars.

Word spread fast in the archaeological community of Egypt, and he had begun to face a significant number of questions as to where these discoveries had been made. Keen to preserve his sites and avoid the competition of less competent and knowledgeable

professionals, he had kept quiet as to the exact locations.

My interest was piqued by his reticence to divulge, and I asked if he could share with me the names of the ancient locations in which his finds had come to light. He hesitated, glancing around the dimly lit room. He appeared on the edge of sharing some information with me when he checked himself, and drew a small piece of paper and a pencil from an inside jacket pocket. He began to make some notes, and passed me the paper when this was done—however, my curiosity was only increased rather than satisfied, as merely the following numbers were written on it:

8 5 12 9 15 16 15 12 9 19

19 1 17 17 1 18 1

20 8 5 2 5 19

1 12 5 24 1 14 4 18 9 1

"These are the names you seek, my friend," he said, "yet in case there are those spying on us even now I am afraid you will need to decode this list to reveal them."

How had the names been encoded, and what names were concealed?

STRANGE RELATIONS

When I visit Cairo, I delight in wandering the corridors of the Egyptian Museum, with its veritable treasure trove of ancient history.

During my most recent visit, I found myself particularly drawn to the papyrus collection. I am perpetually astounded that any of this thin, vulnerable material might have survived, particularly with the vividness the illustrations.

I perused the various scrolls aimlessly, searching for nothing in particular, and being drawn by whatever caught my eye. As I progressed in this fashion, I found myself gazing upon a scroll which seemed to be about a single family. Studying the images and hieroglyphs, I deduced that the male child was the focus of the account. He seemed to be a young boy of around eleven, whose father was a prominent scribe to the pharaoh.

As I read further, I noticed a strange intricacy in the ages of the people described. It seemed that the boy in question's father was in fact older than the boy's grandfather! I considered this for some minutes in a state of puzzlement before clarity descended upon me, and an explanation presented itself.

How could this strange situation be explained?

A DIFFERENT KINGDOM

Lord Carnarvon wrote to me again last week. It seems that, in a divergence from his usual set of interests, he has decided to spend some time reading about the Roman emperors. He explained that he started off reading about the Roman republic, but was (perhaps predictably) then drawn to tales of Mark Anthony and Cleopatra, and how Egypt eventually became a province of the Roman empire.

I must say, this particular period of Egyptian history does not fascinate me nearly so much as the more ancient epochs. However, he did manage to catch my attention by enclosing a puzzle he had cut from the newspaper with his correspondence. It was a small scrap of paper with the following written upon it:

"'BASTET' has none, 'SCARAB' has one,
'CAIRO' and 'LUXOR' have two,
'MEMPHIS', 'PILLAR', 'PYRAMID' and 'RIVAL' all
have three, and 'CIVILIAN' has six.
So how many does 'VICTORY' have?"

I paused for a minute, considering my benefactor's recent pursuits, and it was this that eventually led me to deduce the common feature of the words. I hastily scribbled a reply, including the solution to his problem.

What number did I send as my answer?

A CLASSIFIED TASK

C lassifying artefacts after a discovery is often time-consuming. We are extremely thorough and never rush the process, despite mocking comments by rivals who claim to process artefacts far more swiftly.

I once found myself arguing with an obnoxious archaeologist by the name of Smith, who was confident that his methods were considerably more efficient than mine. He told me that he had a collection of 500 artefacts to categorize.

During our discussion as to who would be the fastest under similar levels of classification detail, he stated that he would pre-sort the objects so that he could work through ten artefacts on the first day, twenty on the second day, thirty on the third day and so on, continuing to log an extra ten artefacts each day.

I, in a somewhat competitive mood, proposed that I would do similarly but—to allow sufficient time to pre-sort—I would log just one artefact on the first day and two on the second day, and then four on the day after that, continuing to double the number of artefacts I logged on each subsequent day.

Using these methods, who would be the first to finish logging the 500 artefacts: Smith or myself? And how many days would it take for the fastest person to finish?

AN UNFORTUNATE INCIDENT

I have been lucky enough not to have caused too many accidents or breakages on my digs. I have, however, heard terrible stories, including one of a priceless papyrus from the ancient world reduced to ash after an accident with a lantern, and another of a centuries-old vase shattered due to a drunken misstep.

Others, however, are not always so careful. The remains of a precious necklace, found deep underground in the Valley of the Kings, was dropped on one recent excavation, with pieces flying off in all directions.

I was most annoyed and soon discerned that there had been four people involved: Hussein, Abdel, Alfred, and Harry. On questioning them to try and work out exactly what had happened, I received four statements:

Harry stated that Abdel had dropped it.
Hussein said only that Harry was telling the truth.
Abdel claimed that Harry had dropped the necklace.
Alfred claimed that Hussein was telling the truth.

Through various other investigations, I ascertained that only one of these statements was true, the rest lies.

Who had dropped the necklace, and who was telling the truth?

THE SPECIALISTS

In my earlier days, before I became involved in working for Lord Carnarvon, my work would often take me to the offices of the Egyptian Antiquities Service where I was employed as their Inspector of Monuments.

On one visit, I decided to take lunch in a cafeteria frequented by specialists in the field of archaeology. I acquired for myself a bowl of soup, and while casting my eyes around the room for somewhere to sit I noticed a few familiar faces: a group of people I knew to be specialists in the field of Egyptology.

I walked over to their table, and was pleased when they invited me to join them. As well as the familiar faces, there were three academic-looking people at the table who were unfamiliar to me. Carl, a prominent specialist in Egyptian death rituals, introduced them as Mary, Albert, and Saleem.

> *"Ah, but Howard, can you guess our fields of specialism?", Mary asked me. "One of us is a specialist in Alexandrian literature; one of us specializes in the history of pyramid construction; and one of us is a specialist in ancient Egyptian cuisine. We will also give you some further*

*information, but not all of us will tell the truth! It
will be an amusing game to play over lunch."*

I felt that my definition of amusing might be a little
different, but as the three began to speak I felt I
should at least try to deduce their various areas of
interest.

*"Saleem is the specialist in Alexandrian literature",
Mary began.*
*"Saleem is a specialist in the history of pyramid
construction", Albert said.*
*"I am a specialist in neither Alexandrian literature
nor the history of pyramid construction", said
Saleem.*

Carl (who I knew to be a truthful source) leaned over
to me, whispering that the person who specialized in
Alexandrian literature was telling the truth.

Which person was a specialist in which field?

THE CARRIAGE CLOCKS

Travelling abroad is in many ways a great equalizer, forcing you to become accustomed to a different environment, and to interact with those who have lived entirely different lives. It encourages one to adopt an open mindset. I am therefore grateful that Lord Carnarvon has not fully inherited that snobbishness which so often accompanies those of the aristocratic classes.

However, there have been occasions when my attention has been drawn to his superior social status. Indeed, last Christmas, my assistant Arthur Callender and I both received a package from the Carnarvons, each containing an ornate carriage clock. The two clocks were slightly different in design, and Arthur, being of an inquisitive and somewhat impudent disposition, asked me one evening which clock I thought to be the more expensive. I am ashamed to say that I agreed to involve myself in a wager to establish this information, whereby Callender would consult with Lady Evelyn to discover how much each clock had cost, and whoever turned out to have the more

expensive clock would have to surrender it to the other. If both clocks transpired to have cost the same amount, we would draw a line under the whole matter and keep our own clocks.

I reasoned (perhaps naively, now I think further on it) that the chances of me having the less expensive clock, were there to be one, was simply 50:50. If it transpired that I had the more expensive clock, causing me to lose the bet, I would lose the value of the clock. However, if I won the bet, I would win the more expensive clock, causing me to gain a clock greater in value than the one I already possessed. With this in mind, I felt confident making the wager since, if I won the bet, my winnings would be greater than the amount I stood to lose if I lost the bet. This felt to me, mathematically speaking, like the right decision.

However, once the bet had been made, I discovered that my friend Callender had reasoned in exactly the same way—so surely we could not both have the upper hand in such a situation?

How do you explain this paradox?

THE BRUSHES

There are many specific tools which are needed for archaeology, all of which must be used with care and attention in order to avoid damaging any of the precious artefacts from the ancient world which may be hiding below the ground.

We have an extensive selection of tools in the Valley of the Kings, which we sometimes attempt to keep  an accurate inventory of—but, with so much else to do, we often lose track and various items inevitably become misplaced. People unintentionally leave small tools in their pockets or knapsacks, and brushes in particular have a habit of vanishing, seemingly into thin air.

One morning, when my team of archaeologists was assembled, I realized that the numbers of brushes relative to those who needed to use them didn't match up. If each archaeologist was given exactly one brush then one archaeologist would not have a brush at all. However, if the archaeologists shared brushes with one brush between two, there would be one brush left over.

How many archaeologists were there in the team, and how many brushes did we have?

THE ARCHER

While investigating a series of cartouches from the reign of the great queen Hatshepsut, I came across an interesting sequence detailing an archery competition.

Two young men of whom the queen was apparently fond had become engaged in a debate about their respective archery skills. They decided to see who could fire the most arrows in just one minute.

One of the men, named Teti, knew that he could fire one arrow every three seconds, taking into account the time it would take him to remove each arrow from its quiver and lodge it into the bow before shooting.

How many arrows could he shoot in just one minute?

PHARAONIC NUMBERING

Lord Carnarvon's visits sometimes provide a strange insight into the world of the British aristocracy; while my mind is full of ancient burial customs and strange gods, he is more often concerned with the management of his large country estate. I am therefore perpetually amazed at the amount of time he still manages to put into his passion for Egyptology.

His visits to Egypt are always a source of pleasure, and when he is in England we continue to exchange missives. In fact, of late, he has rather taken to sending newspaper puzzles to me that he feels are relevant—a rather quirky habit for such a sober man.

Just last week he sent me such a list, which read as follows:

DEDUMOSE I ≈ 9

NEFERKARE VIII ≈ 17

PTOLEMY III ≈ 10

RAMSES II ≈ 8

SHOSHENQ VI ≈ 14

THUTMOSE IV ≈ 12

Luckily I was able to deduce what method had been followed on each line easily enough, and my attentions were not diverted from my studies for more than one or two minutes.

What method had been used to number this list of ancient pharaohs?

THE BOASTFUL ARCHAEOLOGIST

The lengths to which people will go to establish themselves as superior to others truly astonishes me. I was again reminded of this fact while in conversation with a young archaeologist at the Institute of Antiquities in Cairo, just the other day. The son of a wealthy Marquis, he had recently voyaged to Egypt from England, and was determined to establish himself as the most conspicuously successful professional in his field.

To this end, he had begun boasting to everyone he spoke to about how quickly and accurately he could translate and interpret hieroglyphs. I was secretly pleased when a colleague of mine who had found some extremely cryptic inscriptions while investigating a temple in Luxor approached, asking for his help in interpreting. My colleague sketched out a series of hieroglyphs, which I recognized as a puzzle—one which the same colleague had shown to me the previous day. Roughly translated, the puzzle read as follows:

Three animals speak to you, yet only one speaks the truth. This is the spirit of the god who will guide you on your path.

Crocodile: The crocodile is the animal you seek

Cobra: The cobra or the crocodile is the animal you seek

Camel: The cobra or the camel is the animal you seek

I saw the boastful young man grow a deep shade of crimson, a light sweat appearing on his brow as he realized he was out of his depth.

Which animal's statement is true?

THE FORGOTTEN NAME

I am ashamed to admit that, when I get caught up in my work, I am liable to be absent-minded.

Many years ago, I was most embarrassed when I used the wrong name to address a colleague who had recently arrived to help with an excavation. My mortification became more severe when I realized that I could not in fact remember his name at all.

He stood in the doorway in a state of obvious irritation, with his injured pride meaning that he was unwilling to tell me his name.

"Can you at least give me an initial to help my memory on its way?" I hesitatingly enquired. His response was somewhat cryptic:

> *"Fine. I will give you a clue—the rest is up to you."*
> *He continued, "Consider the alphabet as a line of letters, reading A-Z from left to right. My first initial is immediately to the right of the letter which is three to the left of the letter which is midway between the letter which is three to the right of the letter K and the letter which is two to the left of the letter V."*

My heart sank, but I set to work to discover the required letter.

What was the man's first initial?

THE BAKER

There are many ways in which our modern society is tied to that of ancient Egypt. Flour, for example, has not wavered in its importance and indeed, in the market which I often frequent, there are many stalls selling bread in a myriad of forms.

One such bread stall sells dry crispbreads and crackers in different shapes and sizes. While walking past this stall recently, I happened to hear a conversation between a customer and the baker.

It seemed that the customer was in the habit of buying large, flat crispbreads that were 8 inches in diameter. The baker had perfected the art of making these baked goods more or less perfectly circular. However, the baker had run out of this particular product that day. Instead, for each large crispbread that the customer wanted, the baker proposed to sell him two circular crispbreads which were 4 inches in diameter, for the same price as the 8-inch crispbreads.

The customer thought for a moment, and seemed content that he would be receiving the same quantity of the product overall—and yet it caused me to pause and wonder.

Was this a fair deal?

ORGANIZING THE VALLEY

I settled down one evening to read an interesting account of Sir John Garner Wilson, the inventor of the labelling system for the tombs in the Valley of the Kings. Each tomb is labelled in sequence of its discovery, with its number prefaced by the letters "KV", standing for "King's Valley".

I was busy perusing a list of information about the various kings named Ramses who had been discovered in the valley, when I noticed a cryptic message which had been tucked between the pages of the book:

The great god of kingship hides within—
the tombs hide all you need...
but be sure to order the kings from first unto last.

KV4 (Ramses XI)   T F D S L B Q
KV2 (Ramses IV)   U O V G A W N
KV7 (Ramses II)   P T F N A E H
KV6 (Ramses IX)   O R W V Z U D
KV1 (Ramses VII)   R Y E C H J A

After considering the note for some minutes, I managed to reveal the god that was being referenced.

Which god was it?

THE BOOKSHELF

I have an extensive collection of books, and have created a small library for myself in my Egyptian residence.

A key part of my book collection is a three-volume text on hieroglyph translation. Each of the volumes is the same size, and each is 512 pages in length. I store them in a row in the usual order, i.e. with volume one on the left and volume three on the right, with volume two sitting in between. Their spines face outwards and are the right way up, as you would expect. With the ornate decoration on these perfectly coordinated spines, they form a thing of beauty.

You can imagine my consternation when I discovered that a small family of beetles had taken up residence on this shelf. I was furious to discover that the larvae of these beetles had chewed through from the first page of volume one all the way through to the last page of volume three!

I immediately took the books to my desk to assess the damage that had been done. How many book pages, not including covers, had the larvae chewed through?

THE GRANDFATHER CLOCK

I am an advocate of absolute silence while I am working. I find that even the slightest noises can distract me entirely from the work I am doing, and render any attempts at concentration quite useless. It is for this reason that working in public places is usually beyond me—I prefer to be the curator of my working position, finding somewhere where I have the power to eliminate any noises that might occur. However, one cannot always achieve this.

I remember clearly once having to work in a small room in a library, though I cannot immediately recall in which city it was located. As well as the miscellaneous irksome coughs and sighs from the other library users, there was a large grandfather clock in the corner of the room which periodically disturbed me with its chimes. After around an hour of attempting to work, I gave up entirely, and began to contemplate the clock.

I noticed that when the clock struck on the hour, it chimed the appropriate number of chimes to reflect the hour. In addition to this, it struck exactly once whenever it hit a quarter hour—including at thirty minutes past each hour. While I was sat there, I heard the clock strike with a single chime. I wondered, if I was not cognizant of the time, what would be the greatest number of single chimes I would have to hear in order to be certain of the correct time?

How many single chimes would I need to hear, and what is the longest I would have to wait to hear them?

THE SUPERVISOR

Though my influence in the Valley of the Kings has been great, and I have gathered considerable fame from my discoveries—indeed I dare say my words as I peered through the door of Tutankhamun's tomb will go down in history—I find it somewhat galling to be placed under the instruction of others in my own field. However, this was indeed the case when the Department of Antiquities in Egypt sent Pierre Lacau to oversee the process of investigating the tomb of the young pharaoh.

I was sat quietly one evening, enjoying the waning sunlight with a book, when I was disturbed by the footsteps of the irascible Frenchman—he strode up to me with a newspaper under his arm, and struck up conversation. Remembering my colleagues' advice for me to be civil, I replied politely. Yet, in the course of conversation, I could not help myself from asking him how long he intended to remain in the Valley of the Kings. His reply was simultaneously cryptic and infuriating:

"Wouldn't you like to know, Carter! I'll tell you, but only if you can answer me this.

"My newspaper is supposed to be made of twelve sheets of paper, folded in half. On the first folded sheet are pages one, two, forty-seven, and forty-eight. The whole thing is filled with nonsense as I discovered while reading it, but nothing as erroneous as turning to page seventeen and finding that it was missing entirely. And if seventeen was missing, there ought to be three other pages missing, too. Tell me what those other missing pages are, and I'll tell you when I'm back off to Cairo."

I thought quickly, for I was desperately keen to know when I would be rid of him. What other page numbers were on the sheet featuring page seventeen of the newspaper?

THE DATES

Ihave become somewhat partial to dates during my time in Egypt—the fruit, not the calendar event. Indeed, I occasionally bring a bag of them with me to the excavation site for all to share.

On one of these occasions, it seemed that everyone on the site was ravenously hungry, and the bag was nearly finished by the middle of the morning. I noticed that some had stored a quantity of dates in their pockets, and suggested that they negotiate among themselves to divide the produce out equally. A series of conversations ensued, and I began to lose interest in the matter of refreshment. However, I happened to overhear part of a conversation between two workers:

> *"If you give me five of your dates, then we will have an equal number of dates."*

Turning my head to see the quantities of fruit held by each of them, I observed that this statement was true. I also noticed that if, after this transaction had taken place, the first worker had given the five dates back to the second, the second worker would have had twice as many dates as the first.

How many dates did both workers start with?

BURIED ALIVE

Some time ago I was working alongside a specialist who told me a most grisly tale, of a tomb she had been helping to excavate. Within the tomb of this nobleman had been buried some tens of his servants, who the evidence showed had been bricked into the crypt with their deceased master while still alive. I was quite horrified at this idea, and told her that I fortunately had found little evidence of the practice in my time as an archaeologist.

Perhaps in a desire to shift the topic, but without it being too abrupt a transition, she then said to me, "In my line of work, I'm always coming across things which are buried before they're even born, and then dug up again—usually when the diggers are quite sure they are dead. And many a time they are even buried alive."

This sounded equally morbid, but the way she told it to me made me sure this could not be such a violent activity as it sounded, and she assured me that what she described was very commonplace. I might even have been involved in it myself.

What was she describing?

FRACTIONS OF EGYPT

Ionce paid a visit to the vast halls of the British Museum in order to peruse a selection of ancient mathematical documents. In particular, the museum has a fascinating scroll known as the Egyptian Mathematical Leather roll, which shows that the ancient Egyptians had developed a system of fractions.

I found myself standing next to a gentleman who was making extensive notes in a small leather-bound book. They seemed to be numerical in nature, and when I asked as to his purpose I discovered that he was studying the history of mathematics.

Being in an inquisitive frame of mind, I asked if he knew of any interesting problems he could present me with, to which he replied that he had just seen a particularly good one. After some minutes of flicking through the pages of his book, he came up with this:

"What is one half of two-thirds of three-quarters of four-fifths of five-sixths of six-sevenths of seven-eighths of eight-ninths of nine-tenths of one thousand?"

Initially I thought that there was no way I could solve this without copious notes, but then I realized that I could work it out in my head with ease. What is the solution, and how can you work it out without notes or any modern calculating device?

A TIME-CONSUMING CONUNDRUM

When I was a young apprentice I worked alongside an historian who uncovered the remains of an object that I struggled to identify. I asked my co-worker what he thought the artefact might be, at first glance.

"Oh I should think this is quite obvious, no? Look at the shape. You are certainly familiar with them, although they rarely turn up in these excavations."

"Well, then—it must have been useful to someone, or perhaps sentimentally important," I replied, thinking of the unlikeliness of someone wanting to preserve a useless item for centuries.

"Oh absolutely. Very useful indeed. Nowadays, we buy them to eat—but they are never eaten."

I felt my colleague was toying with me.

What had he identified the object as?

THE THEBAN
SENTRY

My career has taken me around many of the ancient cities of Egypt, and I have been astounded by the beauty and variety of the artefacts and remains I have encountered.

The legendary temple of Karnak particularly captured my imagination while I was working in Thebes—the immense columns of the Great Hypostyle Hall are, in my opinion, one of the greatest architectural wonders of the ancient world.

While working in this ancient city, I came across many stories of pharaohs and their military activities. One in particular remains clear in my mind, as it presented something of a puzzle. The hieroglyphs told a tale of a sentry who had been placed on night watch during a time of political unrest in the region. The pharaoh had been confident that some form of attack was imminent and, sure enough, one day at sunrise the sentry had run to the pharaoh, claiming that he had just had a long and troubling dream in which armies were marching from the west, intent on storming the temple.

The great ruler prepared his armies and, as the sun rose higher in the sky, lines of soldiers appeared. Thankfully, as the pharaoh had been forewarned, his troops were able to protect the temple and repel the invasion.

After the noise of battle had died down, the pharaoh approached the sentry who had warned him of the impending threat. However, rather than rewarding him, he threw him into the dungeons of his palace.

Why did the pharaoh act in this way?

THE LINE OF SUCCESSION

In ancient Egypt power was passed down through the bloodlines of powerful families, with pharaohs able to trace their royal lineage throughout the centuries. There are therefore many carefully compiled accounts of the families of kings, and rumours of plots by lesser royals to murder pharaohs to clear their path.

While reading one such document, I read an account of a group of royal women, all of whom were related to one another, although they were not sisters. The names of these four women were Satiah, Iaret, Tiye, and Amenia.

As I read on, the hieroglyphs related that Tiye and Iaret had the same relationship to one another as Satiah and Amenia did to each other. In addition to this, Satiah had the same relationship to Iaret as Tiye did to Satiah.

Remembering that they are not sisters, how were the four women related? The only other information I had was that Tiye was the oldest, and at least one of the women was a mother to one of the others.

THE LIBRARY

As a child growing up in Norfolk, I never expected to one day be living thousands of miles away in Egypt. And yet now I find myself so infrequently in England that I almost feel more at home in the land of pyramids and ancient tombs.

When I do return to England, I occasionally visit a small library not far from my residence. I find it a comforting atmosphere in which to conduct my work, and as it is seldom frequented by others I often have the luxury of the place to myself.

On one evening visit, however, I encountered a gentleman in peculiar circumstances. I had opened the door of a small anteroom in the library, which I knew to contain a desk and a comfortable leather armchair. It was entirely dark, with no electric light, candles or lamps within, and the curtains were drawn so as to extinguish the light of the moon. I lit a lamp, preparing to get myself situated, when I saw that a man was sat at the desk, reading a book. Once I had got over my initial shock, I wondered how he was reading without any source of illumination.

How could this be done?

A PARTY AT HIGHCLERE

The parties of the English aristocracy are often a mystery to me. Sometimes I feel there is nothing worse than spending an evening with a group of landed peers, talking of property, inheritance, society scandal—and little else.

Lord Carnarvon once told me about a dinner party he threw at Highclere Castle, his estate in Hampshire. I admit I had been only half-listening, and had asked without much real interest how many guests had attended. With a glint in his eye, he had responded that present at the party had been one grandmother, one grandfather, two mothers, two fathers, two husbands, two wives, one mother-in-law, one father-in-law, four children, two sons, two daughters, one sister, two brothers, and three grandchildren. "Gosh. That's quite a crowd!" I had commented.

> *"Ah, but not as many as you might imagine", Carnarvon had replied. "Of course, all men are sons and grandsons, and all women are daughters and granddaughters, but I have counted only those relationships which were actually present at the party."*

Given the relationships described, what is the smallest number of people that could have been present at the party?

MISCHIEVOUS TWINS 2

Some time ago, I had the strange experience of conversing with Ammon and Baahir, twins from Cairo who, while working in the Valley of the Kings, were fond of trying to perplex their colleagues by sometimes deliberately lying.

I found myself in the same tomb complex as the pair again recently, and discovered in the course of conversation that they had chosen a new strategy for the current month. They had decided that every statement Ammon made on Mondays, Tuesdays and Wednesdays would be a lie, but he would always tell the truth the rest of the week. Baahir, on the other hand, would always lie on Thursdays, Fridays and Saturdays, but always tell the truth for the other days of the week.

During our conversation, Ammon commented that he had been lying yesterday. Baahir retorted that he had been lying yesterday as well.

Who was telling the truth, and on what day did the conversation take place?

THE DREAM

I am often branded as a solitary, misanthropic sort, especially by those who have only heard of me through the social grapevines of England—but the fact is that settled family life has never much appealed to me. I would rather spend my days engaged in the study of ancient inscriptions and votive offerings than love and the ways of women.

This said, there are some family relationships which I find charming to observe—the young Lady Carnarvon and her father, for example, share a most tender and affectionate bond. It is a delight to witness their shared enthusiasm for ancient Egypt when they visit the sites they sponsor, and the joy they both take in the other's interest.

One afternoon, while the three of us were taking lunch together, Lady Evelyn began to recount a strange tale she had learned of through one of her acquaintances back in England. The acquaintance, a young countess, had become engaged to a man prone to vivid nightmares, who often started awake in the middle of the night screaming in response to macabre situations.

This man had been staying at the family home of his future wife, occupying the room next door to

hers. Evelyn recounted that one night the unfortunate man had dreamed that he was trapped inside one of the great pyramids of Giza, and was being pursued around its gloomy corridors by a mummy, reanimated by some powerful occult force. He had found his way into a small chamber, and discovered an inscription of what looked like a spell—yet before he could decipher it in the dim light, the form of the mummy filled the doorway and he was trapped. Hearing the cries of anguish coming from the next room, the young countess had dashed through the door to shake him awake. However, before he could regain consciousness, he dropped dead.

"My dear, I fear someone has played a cruel trick on you with this tale," laughed Lord Carnarvon once his daughter had finished her account.

Why did Carnarvon not believe the tale that Lady Evelyn had been told?

FAMILY TREES

As I took a walk along the Nile on an extended break from some excavation work one day, I was grateful for the plentiful shade of the trees which grow along the riverside. The verdant embankment was only made possible by the life-giving waters of the magnificent river, and stood in stark contrast to the Valley of the Queens, where my morning work had taken me.

But one type of tree does still exist in the Valley of the Queens: the family tree. Years of family history—of ancestors, descendants, and the most noble lineages—are encased within the walls there.

This morning I had come across an inscription on a piece of stone, detailing the relationships of some of the residents interred within. Alas, time had worn away much of the writing, and only a few remnants of the text were still visible to modern eyes. After some tricky transliteration of the hieroglyphs, I uncovered the following:

... ~ my aunt, who has a sister that is not my aunt ~ ...

...and then the rest of the text is lost to history.

Hours later, as I strolled along the banks of the river, I thought long and hard about who this sister must have been; this sister who lived so many centuries ago. What might her life have been like, noble as her family must have been?

And what, indeed, was this sister's relationship to the writer of this fragment of family history?

DISTRACTION TECHNIQUES

There was a supervisor on the excavations of Tutankhamun's tomb who could be exceedingly tiresome when he wished, making no pretence at trying to be civil. At such distance from London it was difficult to replace staff, and on occasion I despaired that our work would sometimes require us to spend considerable amounts of time in close quarters.

However, I was cheered when I realized that he was easily distracted by problems and puzzles involving numbers. As a result, I have kept an eye out for conundrums I can throw his way, as one might give sweets to a child to distract it.

The latest puzzle I thought of myself and it was, in my opinion, rather clever. I asked him to take the digits from one to nine and, using each digit only once, form a sequence of three three-digit numbers where the second number was double the first, and the third number was three times the first number.

Can you find such a sequence? And then can you find three more that also fulfil the requirements?

THE PUBLISHER

In order to share our experiences in Egypt more easily and in more detail, Lord Carnarvon and I decided to write a book. Having secured a publisher and a selection of academics to assist with the process, we set to work describing our finds.

When the finished copies eventually arrived, I commented to Carnarvon on the intricate lettering that comprised the chapter numbers. While contemplating how this effect had been achieved, Carnarvon posed an interesting question:

"There are fourteen chapters in total in this book. Now, if the numbers one to fourteen, written out in words as in the book, had been printed using movable type, then how many individual letter blocks would be needed? Remember that, although the blocks can be re-used for different numbers, that for each individual chapter number all of the letters are printed simultaneously, so you will need for example two 'e's for the number 'three'."

Later, at leisure, I put my mind to this calculation. What was my eventual response?

STONE RIDDLES

Occasionally, on the walls of a previously-undisturbed tomb, one stumbles across an inscription in the doorway. A warning, perhaps, or simply a signpost, letting you know whose resting place you have come across. They are quite awesome to behold, these messages from millennia ago, despite their significance not being immediately apparent to modern eyes.

They are, of course, eventually meticulously recorded and then scheduled for translation, and often a rough sketch or two is made on the spot so that the message may be revealed as soon as is possible.

I once encountered such an inscription in the dark antechamber of a rather small tomb, whose meaning I spent some time later attempting to decipher in the hot sun. There were in fact two puzzles for me to solve that day since, once I had uncovered the senses of the glyphs themselves, the content of the inscription appeared to be a riddle. Perhaps, like the mighty Sphinx, this writer was hoping for an exchange of intellect before allowing entry to the place within.

Written on the wall was the following:

I lived when
there was light
But died
when it was shone
upon me

With some trepidation, we had unsealed the door to find that, bizarrely, the tomb was empty. Nobody, it seemed, had been interred there. If the inscription had not referred to a person, then what *did* it mean?

I sat for a while, puzzling in the midday sun as it crossed over the valley I was working in. Eventually the answer came to me. Can you think of what phenomenon this archaic enigma referred to?

OUT OF DEPTH

Ah, the Nile. As vibrant today as it ever was, in spite of the many attempts to tame it. Still it courses on through the desert, delivering life to the parched surroundings, carving a path of oases and emerald embankments.

Excavations are always subject to dither and delay, and on days when no digging can be done I sometimes take a trip down to the river to take in the surroundings, and leave the tombs behind me. I often find myself lost in thought on these trips, with very little to shake me from my musings on the past.

On a recent outing I was distracted by pondering the ancient irrigation systems put in place by those who lived off the land, but at some point I refocused on the river and realized, to my horror, that there was someone stuck in the river, almost submerged in the water. Upon closer inspection, however, the person in question was showing no signs of distress. In fact, they seemed to be taking a cooling dip in the water, an understandable response to the day's relentless heat. They had clearly calculated their trajectory and waded far enough that they might be largely covered by the cooling currents, and yet could still maintain a secure

foothold on the bed of the river itself, stopping them from being washed away. Clearly this was not their first sun-defying submersion.

Once their safety had been established, I asked myself how this person had managed to guarantee that they would not succumb to the currents of the river, and then reminded myself of an undeniable fact: no matter how deep the water, how fast the flood, or how steady the stream, there is always a limit on how far one could travel into the mighty river. What is the furthest anyone can wade into the Nile?

THE JOURNAL

I have found that keeping a journal is a useful way for me to keep track of my activities in Egypt. By jotting down a few notes each day, I can record all of my discoveries and be confident that in the future I will have an accurate account of the date and location of the find.

I am usually meticulous in labelling my journal entries, and like to begin each one with a note of the day of the week, the date and the time of writing. However, when flicking back through the pages of my latest journal, I discovered that the day of the week label was missing from the last day of January. I was easily able to fill in the blank using my labelling of surrounding days, of course, but as I was reading my other entries from that month I noticed that in that particular January there had been exactly four Tuesdays and exactly four Fridays. I further realized that it would also have been perfectly possible to use this information alone to fill in the blank.

What day of the week was it on the 31st of January of the year in question?

THE SHATTERED BOX

It is often commented that the vividness of Egyptian artworks are phenomenally well-preserved. Indeed, the dramatic kohl-outlined eyes of painted statues have a stare that is as penetrating today as it would have been thousands of years ago.

However, these vibrant artefacts are as fragile as they are beautiful, and many have been damaged over the centuries by robbers. I remember once entering an anteroom only to find a small, painted box, perhaps once a chest for holding jewellery, shattered into many pieces. The pieces had fallen so that some painted faces were visible, while other faces lay so that they revealed the wood beneath.

While looking upon this sorry item, I contemplated exactly how many pieces would, in general, have at least one painted face if an arbitrary item was split apart.

Take a 3 x 3 x 3-inch cube, for example, painted on all but the top side. If it was split apart into twenty-seven equally sized cubes, how many of these smaller cubes would have at least one painted face on them?

THE SOUND OF
SILENCE

To be honoured with the excavation of the Valley of the Kings is not something I take for granted. Indeed, it is a privilege to be one of the first people since ancient times to discover the resting places of these monarchs, and indeed their sons and brothers. To be in the presence of these bygone rulers, even in death, is quite something—I am in no doubt as to how rare and fascinating a position I am in, as a detective of history.

In spite of the treasures and the opulence which regularly greet us, perhaps the most intriguing marvel which strikes me upon the discovery of a new tomb is the silence that has lain within for centuries—the peace, the quiet, and the solitude of its resident, undisturbed for an age. To think that I might be the first living soul in so many years to utter a word aloud in such a chamber, and break the tranquillity of a thousand years, is quite something. I confess that I feel a responsibility to make these first words worthy of their monumental office.

My speech, of course, receives no reply from the inhabitants, and it is a strange thing to always speak first and hear no response. I mentioned this to a fellow excavator, who encouraged me instead merely to be grateful for the unique opportunities I had been afforded, which I suppose is wise counsel indeed. He asked, if I were going to be so churlish, whether I would rather be one who never speaks first, but always replies. I considered my position and saw that  I did indeed have the favourable end of the bargain, not least as I could not think of such a situation as he imagined it. My colleague laughed, and told me it was not so unheard of—but try as I might, I couldn't uncover his meaning.

Can *you* think of something which will always reply, but never be the first to speak?

DUNG BEETLES

The scarab is a familiar sight to all who have studied the ancient world, since this humble, dung-rolling beetle was seen as a symbol of rebirth. The way in which they roll dung across the sand, to create a place to lay eggs, brought the sun god Ra to the ancient Egyptians' minds. Ra was the great deity who rolled the sun across the sky, giving life to the world with its light and warmth.

These small insects can still be seen in Egypt, industriously working to feed themselves and their young. I observed three of them while I was enjoying lunch just last week, with their positions forming a triangle on the sandy ground. They seemed to be yet to decide which direction to roll their various balls in— and so as I ate, I considered the probability of the beetles colliding as they journeyed with their dung.

Simplifying the puzzle somewhat, if the three dung beetles each started at one corner of a hypothetical triangle, then randomly chose one side of the triangle to roll their ball of dung along, what would be the probability that a collision would take place?

THE FRESH-FACED ASSISTANT

The discovery of Tutankhamun's tomb naturally necessitated a great deal of work, and I quickly realized that I would not be able to accomplish the necessary excavation with my team alone. Thankfully, a group from the Metropolitan Museum was working not too far away at the time, and I was able to borrow some of their number.

One of these men was a particularly young-looking man—indeed he seemed to my eyes to be no more than sixteen or seventeen. However, when I (perhaps impertinently?) enquired as to his age, he was adamant that he was similar in age to his much older-looking colleagues.

I have an unfortunate tendency to need to discover exact information, and I am slightly ashamed to say that I pressed him further on the subject, only to be rewarded with a cryptic explanation:

"My age is a two-digit number which is equal to three times the sum of its two digits."

How old was the youthful-looking gentleman?

THE FALL

I am apt to wax lyrical about modern lighting—you may be familiar with the theme already—but no technology, however great, is without its flaws. Indeed, I was using my electric hand-held light just yesterday in the excavation of a set of steps, grateful for the light it afforded me as I approached the bottom of the staircase and descended towards the door of the crypt below. Alas, I slipped on a little loose rubble and, as the ground gave way beneath me, I dropped my illuminator, which suddenly went out with a flash. My own silly fault, and now I was without a light.

Scrabbling around in the dark is not something one wishes to be doing as an archaeologist—with priceless treasures to be found at every turn it really does help to see what one is doing, lest there be some unintended disturbance to the site or its contents. Still, the light had to be located and, if at all possible, switched back on.

When I had recovered the item from the bottom of the sandy steps it was, as I feared, completely out of commission and would provide no more guidance for this particular dig. I wondered how something so useful could be so easily broken, having dropped only a few steps in height—it was hardly a great fall after all. The torch suddenly seemed so evanescent in the company of other ancient objects which had stood the test of the eons, resilience incarnate. Idly, I wondered to myself which items might be the hardiest in the tomb we were about to uncover— perhaps decorative items of alabaster, or tall stone statues of gods and kings?

Some weeks later, as I looked out on an unusually gloomy day, I realized that there was something extremely common which can fall from great heights, and yet never suffers damage upon hitting the ground. I wondered that it had not occurred to me before, but then the majesty of the ancient world does have a habit of overwhelming one's senses.

What extraordinary, yet ordinary matter do you think I was musing upon?

EPHEMERA

Many years ago, when I was little more than a boy, I accompanied other notable archaeologists on their own digs in Egypt, recording the items they discovered in their excavations with the same care and attention with which I undertake it today. Meticulous as I may have been in my methods, the wonder of the task did not escape me. It is easy at any age to be enthralled by these mighty objects and murals, especially those artefacts which were clearly so precious to their owners that they wished to be interred alongside them. And that's quite aside from the canopic jars.

It struck me then that we were seeing a careful curation of the belongings of these long-dead citizens, objects of such beauty and utility to their owners that they needed to be preserved for eternity and perhaps beyond. Naturally, we rarely throw away those things which are most useful to us and are apt to keep them with us in case of future need, and I remarked on this one day to my then-employer. He laughed, noting that I was quite right, and it was unlikely that anyone might want to take a worn-out shoe into the afterlife, or a short-lived woven basket. These things must have been

cast out when they were no longer useful, and hence we often see only the treasures of the past on these digs, and not the well-worn ephemera.

So profound was this musing that I continued the rest of my afternoon's work in some silence. Later, though, I ascertained there was certainly at least one object I could think of that must have been thrown away when it was most needed—and recouped when its usefulness was at an end—which would have been true in the past as much as it still is in the present. But what object do you think I might have been contemplating?

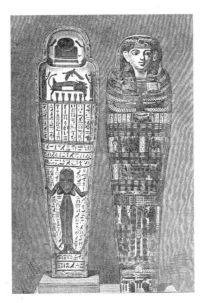

THE SPHINX

The legendary Sphinx is known for her obscure riddles, designed to catch out those who cross her path. I have seen the Great Sphinx of Giza for myself, and can well believe the fear that would be struck into the heart of any who saw this great winged creature in the flesh.

I read a legend once of a traveller who had encountered a sphinx deep in the desert, far from the comforting rush of the Nile. He had been travelling for weeks, and had long since lost track of what day of the week it was. The sphinx had spotted him from afar, and encircled him with her lion's tail, eager for a meal. There was no escape unless the traveller could answer her riddle.

She spoke with a deep, honeyed voice:

"Wanderer, I see your confusion and bewilderment, caused by the heat of the sun and your long journey—but fear not, for I will tell you what day it is. If yesterday were tomorrow, today would be Tuesday."

What day of the week was it, according to the Sphinx?

THE WRITING ON THE WALL

To uncover the door of a tomb is an extraordinary thing—it is hard to describe the moment, after a long search, when the dust is swept away and the seals, signs and symbols are revealed. It is fortunate indeed that the doors to several tombs were labelled with names by some historical hand, that we might more easily discover the identity of the person whose remains lie within. There is no feeling quite like that which occurs when one unveils the name of a king whose name might not have been spoken aloud at that location for many centuries.

One naturally comes across other writings on the walls in this city of the dead—some gilt and splendorous, others scratched into plaster; scribbled graffiti from long ago. I wonder if those illicit writers, like those who decorated the walls of the city of Pompeii, knew that their words might be preserved for thousands of years or more.

But I digress. I once came across such a message in a necropolis and was fortunate enough to be accompanied by a linguist whose mastery of the hieroglyphs meant that she could translate the inscription on the spot. According to her wisdom, the message read:

I disappear the moment
I am shared;
I cease to be whenever
I am aired.

This version, I presumed, involved some poetic license from the translator, but I enjoyed her rendering nonetheless. That said, I couldn't fathom the true meaning of this riddle at all. I knew I had nothing to fear from this enigmatic passage, but I wanted to know what we were dealing with all the same.

Can you interpret what it was that the writing on the wall described?

LOST IN TRANSLATION

Some of my first work in Egypt was that of a transcriber, scrupulously copying out mural inscriptions from recently-discovered tombs, that they might be recorded properly and translated for future understanding. It was there, under the watchful mentorship of my patron, that I developed my passion for the methodical, and a certain dedication to the systematic ways of the archaeologist.

I was once tasked with the copying out of a curious papyrus scroll, which had been found alongside other priceless treasures on a local dig. I was characteristically pedantic in my notation, wishing that no human error on my part might creep into the great work of translating the words of the past. Later on, I looked back at some of my notes and compared them against the work of a translator, who I knew was an esteemed linguist in the company. Looking at his version, however, there seemed to be some serious logical holes in the writing. Whether

the flaws were part of the original text, or had crept in as a cross-language issue, was not clear to me, but nonetheless I felt a duty to question their work.

Tactfully, I began:

"But sir, look here. This passage cannot be logical. This text seems to be describing the relations of some notable courtiers to the king, including this, his doctor, as you have translated. But look, it says that when the brother of the physician died that the king lost some faith in the doctor's practice— as you might expect—but look here—this second part of the text clearly states that this deceased man, the brother of the doctor, had no brother at all. So where, indeed, has this meaning been lost?"

Suffice to say that the translator was not best pleased with my interfering, and immediately proved, rather bluntly, that it was my own inference that was quite incorrect, and not his translation.

Upon further inspection, I saw that he was quite right, and I wrong. Can you see how such a situation between this doctor and this brother-with-no-brother might arise?

THE COUNTESS'S TRICK

On one of her visits to Egypt with her father, Lady Evelyn told me a story of a countess whom she had met at a soirée at Highclere. This lady was notorious for being extremely glamorous, and always had the latest fashions from Paris. However, it seemed that this notoriety had given her some anxiety about preserving her beauty and, at least as Lady Evelyn recounted, she had expressed a terror of growing old.

Lady Evelyn related that she had tried to comfort the countess with suitable compliments, and in the course of their conversation, had then enquired as to the countess's age. She had replied with what I found to be quite a clever trick:

> *"My dear", the aristocratic lady had said, "I am thirty-two years old, so long as you don't count Wednesdays, Fridays or Sundays."*

How old was the countess?

SACRED BIRDS

Thoth was the Egyptian god of wisdom and magic, a great scribe with the head of an ibis. This curved-beaked bird gained great status as a sacred animal as a result of its connection with the god. Many ibis mummies have been discovered in Egypt, presumably all long-ago sacrifices to appeal to Thoth.

Alas, the majestic ibis can be found in Egypt no longer, so my consideration of the species is limited to specimens long dead and mummified. I remember speaking once with an Egyptian scholar in Cairo, and asking if he had ever seen one. He told me that he had in fact come across a flock during his travels in southern Africa. While we were speaking, he also told me of a puzzle he had learned, connected to the sacred species:

"If there are more ibises in the world than there are feathers on any single ibis, and there are no ibises which are completely featherless, then it's a certainty that there will be at least two ibis birds with the same number of feathers, somewhere in the world."

He continued, "Now tell me: is this statement true or false?"

How should I answer?

THE UNENDING
QUEST

It is thanks only to the faith of my patrons that I was finally able to uncover some of the greatest mysteries of the Valley of the Kings—their patience was the key to that final, fateful excavation which uncovered the most famous tomb of all, that of the young Tutankhamun.

The wait for discovery was—at times—agonizing, and there were naturally questions raised about the veracity of such a tomb's existence, shrouded as it was in rumour and mystery. I admit now that I once or twice even privately wondered at its actuality myself.

Of course, by fate and by fortune, we finally came across the fabled shrine and the rest, as they say, is history. Our quest for the tomb was at an end—and now the real work of its unpacking could begin. At long last, an achievement—an objective met—could be written down and sent back home as news.

I recall that on one occasion, in those darker days before our dramatic discovery, I began to wonder at other archaeological missions which were undertaken

seemingly without end—the spurious quests for cities of gold, perhaps, or islands sunk beneath the seas and said to contain submerged treasures. It struck me that there is always one elusive destination, one legendary locale on this earth that one can never reach—no matter how long you spend your days walking directly towards it.

It wasn't a comforting thought, I confess—and I'm rather glad we found the tomb in the end, lest we had added our hunt to a list of endless expeditions. Can you imagine which unreachable place I had been thinking of, in my private despair?

SEEING IS BELIEVING

There is no doubt that the drama and notoriety of some of my discoveries has afforded me some small personal fame among the public and, regrettably, the press. Occasionally, and much to my distain, I am crudely referred to as a "treasure hunter". I assure you there can be nothing more irksome than this—to reduce my life's work to that of a mindless, map-less marauder—but there is little I can do about it. Treasure is, I suppose, the substance of much of my profession.

Occasionally when meeting with other excavators the discussion does turn to the more material, and then there are boasts and brags about the greatest pieces a digger might have discovered. I find it rather crass, but there is some academic interest in the subject, so I do tune in.

During one event, I distinctly remember one scholar whose speciality had not been Egypt but in fact a people who lived a little further from the pyramids, in ancient Sumer. He had studied their lives and their deaths, their scripture and their society, and naturally he had all sorts of fascinating stories to tell about his findings. I recall, however, that he said the greatest treasure he and his team had found in their studies

was not material treasure at all, but wisdom which had been long ago lost, and then rediscovered as their writings were translated into our own tongue. The people, he said, had a propensity for the enigma, and he regaled us with a story of one such puzzle that he had had the pleasure of translating. Said he:

> *"The riddle goes a little like this: Imagine a house, where one enters it sightless, and leaves it able to see. What might it be?"*

After some silly quips about ancient optometrists, the group fell silent as each academic tried to respond first to the age-old wisdom. I wasn't so childish as to shout out my response, but I was pleased that I did in fact manage quickly to generate what I felt was an appropriate solution to the conundrum. Can you?

A DIVIDED KINGDOM

Problems with transferring power from generation to generation are centuries old. Much like modern families, the ancient pharaohs often had trouble deciding what each of their children would stand to inherit after their deaths.

I once read of a noble family who owned many acres of valuable land, planted with barley and the aquatic sedge from which papyrus is made. There were two children in the family who were to inherit the land and yet, when the time came to work out the details of the inheritance, things became somewhat complex.

The children's father, a nobleman who was close to the pharaoh, wanted to divide his land fairly between his two children. However, the path of the Nile and distribution of the fields meant that there was no clear way to divide the land into two equal halves.

Thankfully the nobleman was a philosophical man, and approached the problem as such. He sketched out a map of his land, considered it carefully, and then eventually came up with a neat solution which would ensure that both children would be content with their share of the land.

What solution do you think he devised to ensure that both children were satisfied that the land was divided fairly between them?

ANCIENT NUMBERS

I was once reading a scroll of papyrus which detailed the taxation levied on a large farm, a prolific producer of grain.

As I read, I began absent-mindedly jotting down numbers in my notebook, confident as ever that my haphazard scrawls would be completely comprehensible when I returned to them at a later date. Naturally this was not the case, and I found when I read through my notebook later that evening I could make little sense of what I had written.

However, in the process of going through my notes, I did spot an interesting numerical feature that had arisen, formed where I had written various numbers too close together on the page.

I had created a ten-digit number in which the first digit described the number of zeros in the number, the second digit described the number of ones in the number, the third digit the number of twos, the fourth digit the number of threes, and so on until the tenth digit described the number of nines in the number.

What number had I created from my insufficiently precise note-taking?

A CHAGRIN

O n slow days, or in the aftermath of disappointing
discoveries, I am reminded of a find I made years
ago, before I was trusted enough to carry out my
own excavation work. In the annex of a tomb which
had been largely cleared I discovered a heavy box,
apparently made of solid gold, so fine was the gilding
to the outside. In the soft lights we had rigged to
illuminate the tomb I could almost see my own face in
its golden facade. It had been beautifully preserved,
and I was ostensibly in the presence of treasure.

Set into the gold was a large cartouche, which had
been inscribed atop the lid. The lead archaeologist
on the dig was confident enough in his study that he
thought he might translate the writing on the spot.
It was, it seemed, a label for the box, describing the
contents held within. Part of the writing read as
follows:

Needed by the rich and owned by the poor; Older than time, yet deadly when drunk for too long.

The translator didn't seem to think it was part of a curse, which we found reassuring, although whatever the message meant I'm sure it was intended as a deterrent. Nevertheless, the box was carefully opened, regardless of the apparent warning on the top.

I peered in as the cover was raised, unsure of what might be found within. As a novice, I was rather hoping it might boost my academic standing in the eyes of my mentor, to have found a priceless and unexpected treasure on his dig.

What do you think we found in the box?

CONTENTS

Pots, jars, and boxes with enigmatic contents must be opened carefully when the time is right. Spilling the contents might have disastrous consequences for us as historians and, perhaps, their original owners in the afterlife.

Just the other day I uncovered a curious box when unpacking a tomb, which was soon deemed safe to open. Alas, time seemed to have destroyed much of the contents, but there was a small papyrus scroll inside which I hoped might prove illuminating. I wondered what we might be dealing with, and sought help to determine what clues we had as to the treasures the box might once have held.

I passed the writings onto a translator, who confirmed that the hieroglyphs did indeed give more details on the items which were in the box. There seemed to be a list of comparisons, or measurements of some kind, though of what the measurements pertained to I had no idea. Unfortunately, the text itself was not explicit, and the translator eventually uttered the following:

"Thin is quick, and fat is slow... then later on it seems, ah yes, that short is old, and tall is young."

"I see," I said, although I didn't really see at all. In fact, this rather sounded like nonsense to me. Unfortunately my colleague seemed to think this description entirely solved the mystery of what was in the box, and I was too embarrassed to ask what he thought it meant, so I thanked him for his work.

"Not at all", replied the translator, and he went away, leaving me none the wiser.

So now I ask you: what do you think the box once held?

LIFE AND DEATH

In this line of work, one is never far from death—whether as an occupational hazard in precarious digs, or simply by the very nature of archaeology. And yet, while I uncover the evidence of the departed souls buried here, all around are signs of their life—their families, treasured possessions, adventures, and stories—and of course, their wishes for the journey into the afterlife.

I mentioned this to a colleague one morning, being as I was quite overcome with awe at the magnitude of it all. In an attempt to dam my deep deliberations, he put the following puzzle to me, as we walked along the desert valley.

> *"The Nile is certainly a giver of life, but not all things flourish under its power. While crops and trees might be sustained by its watery might, there are other phenomena which can be entirely destroyed by it.*
>
> *What will grow plentifully with the right supply of food, but will die forever when watered?"*

What indeed?

TRANSLITERATION

Hieroglyphics never cease to fascinate me. They are the keys to the ancient world contained within pictures; the stories told without words; the sounds captured in stone. It is a miracle indeed that we are able to uncover the meanings of these symbols—and yet still today some mystery remains.

To help me with occasional work in translating and transliterating hieroglyphs, I find it most useful to carry an English dictionary around with me. One should always have a reference book on hand to make sure there's no room for error.

Like any book, however, my dictionary is the work of a human being, and human errors are bound to creep in. I notice these little mistakes from time to time: a missing letter, a word in the wrong place, a definition which does not match the meaning I know to be true.

In fact, there is one interesting nuance which I have noticed in my own dictionary and, upon inspection, also appears in the dictionaries of my linguistically inclined colleagues. There is, I fear to say, one word that is always spelled erroneously in *every* English dictionary!

What is it?

THE PRINCESS'S TALE

I was once in the company of an historian whose business was the folklore of ancient civilizations, and whose work was naturally quite fascinating, if rather harder to characterize than that of an archaeologist such as myself. She told me of a tale she had once had the pleasure of translating from an ancient script not unlike hieroglyphs, concerning a young princess and that timeless trope, forbidden love.

The historian told me that this misadventure had been written out on the walls of an ancient city— presumably after decades of being told aloud—so that its meaning might serve as a warning to others who had similar ideas. The princess had fallen in love with a young farmer and the prospect of their relationship was, by all accounts, an inappropriate match for someone of her status. Her father, the monarch of the land, felt so strongly about it that he decreed that this farmer should never look directly at his daughter again, on pain of death.

The duo were naturally rather disheartened at this development but, as the story goes, the princess came up with a plan so that the farmer and she might see one another again. Cryptically, she told him that there was just a small undertaking standing between them, and that he need only solve a puzzle to prove himself worthy of seeing her face again. He needed to find something of hers, said she, that was often seen in water, though it could never get wet. When he had found this mysterious thing, he would be able to look at her without fear.

The young farmer never did solve the riddle, and so he never saw his beloved princess again. If anything, the tale seems to be something of an advert for the necessity of mental acuity rather than a deterrent against illicit affairs, but that rather detracts from the romance of it all, I suppose. I didn't mention this to the historian, and she continued by asking me what I thought the riddle might have meant, and what the boy could have found so that he might look upon the princess once more.

What do you think I said?

THE TROUBLE WITH TWO

Often, as we unpack the halls of antiquity, we come across items which confound us as historians. I once happened upon an intriguing piece of papyrus which seemed to have been designed to lay out clearly the relations of some noble princes to one another—a document concerning one family's particular ancestry.

A particularly befuddling passage, however, concerned the history of two brothers, residents of this land many centuries ago. When the glyphs were fully translated, we realized that these two brothers had been born on the same day, of the same year, to the same mother.

"Twins!", I said aloud—but the translator I was working with was not convinced. In fact, according to their interpretation, the papyrus stated clearly that these brothers—born on the same day, of the same year, to the same mother—were not twins at all.

The translator is a highly respected member of our team but I felt sure that he must have made a mistake in his work. How on earth could these two brothers not have been twins, knowing what we knew about their shared life?

FLIGHT OF FANCY

On a recent excavation I was joined by an ornithologist, whose expertise had been sought to identify some of the fauna which had recently been depicted on long-hidden murals.

Birds of all kinds could be found immortalized on the walls all around us, their feathers gilded and glittering in the lights of the torches we used. The array of wildlife which was once worshipped and revered by those who lived here millennia ago was so ornately depicted that the ornithologist had no trouble in successfully recognizing individual species: here an eagle, there an ibis, and even occasionally a magnificent ostrich.

In a reflective moment, on a walk between tombs, my companion turned to me and said:

"But of course, the fastest flyer in ancient Egypt had no wings at all. Feathers, certainly, but no wings."

At first, I thought she must have been speaking of some absurd, historical peregrine falcon!—but she assured me that this flyer was, in fact, not a bird at all. I pondered for a while at her suggestion, asking myself what on earth she could be hinting at.

At long last, the answer came to me. Can you guess what my collaborator was speaking of?

THE BLOCKS

I came across, long ago, a tomb whose entrance had been marked by a stack of granite blocks. I say marked but, really, the stones had been an excellent way to obstruct our entrance to the crypt altogether—indeed at first they seemed to be impossible to move. Whoever was interred behind the stack clearly had no interest in receiving guests.

Still, we had been tasked with excavating the crypt beneath, and the blocks had to go. Clearly there had been some similar attempts in the past which had been abandoned, for what I assume began as a perfect cube formation had been reduced to a misshapen stack of blocks, with single stones removed from various layers of the structure, seemingly without any deliberate design.

I estimated that it would take an hour to remove each block, with the correct leverage and equipment. My colleague and I then calculated how long it would take for the whole structure to be dismantled and, alas, came to quite different numbers.

Can you determine for yourself how many blocks were left, and therefore how many hours would it take to clear the lot? There were—of course—no floating blocks in the stack. More's the pity; it would have made the job far easier.

A BREAKTHROUGH

No matter how careful we are in unpacking a tomb, we are sure to come across broken items. Some damage is the work of graverobbers, who existed in antiquity just as much as they do today, while other damage is the work of time itself—the slow erasure of form and function caused by the mere passing of the years. But some pieces are so fragile that, regrettably, their very rediscovery is a hazard to them, such as ancient fabrics which crumble to dust at the merest touch.

I occasionally remember that old optimistic expression, that even a stopped clock is correct twice a day, and wonder which of these items might still retain some of their original functionality, even where they have defects today. Indeed, minor imperfections need not hamper the utility of a well-made object, and in fact at a particular point this very morning I found myself considering a most common object which *must* be broken if one is to extract its most useful qualities.

Can you imagine which item I might have been thinking of?

SEE AND BE SEEN

We are fortunate indeed to live in the age of the electric light.

When uncovering tombs, a candle is useful indeed to detect any hazardous or tainted airs which might have been sealed within for millennia. But the electric torch—a marvellous invention—tends to best show off the beauty hidden within a newly opened tomb, illuminating the gaps around part-sealed doorways. And finally, when the meticulous work of logging a tomb's artefacts begins, a complete circuit of electric lights allows the task to continue deep into the evening.

I never know what will be found when light finally shines into a long-sealed interior. I am often surprised by the scale of some of the items within, with huge chariots and statues that seem at odds with the low ceilings and indeed the clandestine nature of the crypts themselves. They grow taller and more majestic as we unveil them in the light of our torches.

I realize, of course, that there are some things which do the opposite—that is, that they become smaller as everything else becomes more illuminated and easier to see.

To what phenomenon am I referring?

APPRENTICES

I am quite happy to work alone when it is practical: I have a rather particular style of study and the more interferences to my process that can be avoided, the better.

Last week I was, however, joined on a particular task by a fellow archaeologist and, while I did not really mind their presence and input, they did have a rather annoying apprentice in tow, who did nothing but disrupt the day's work with his questions and queries. Curiosity is the natural state of any historian, I concede, but quiet reflection is also a highly prized aptitude and I wish he had had some more experience of it.

The boy had a hundred questions about the tombs I had uncovered in my career and, at one point in the day the discussion turned to the tomb of Tutankhamun, which it often does when I meet people for the first time. He was most interested in the unbroken seal of the inner tomb, a twist of rope which had been untouched by human hands for a few thousand years. He had clearly seen a photo of the seal and, while we were working, had been trying to recreate it with a piece of string he had found on site. He was rather easily distracted and, far from listening closely to my tales of the inner shrines of the tomb, he interrupted to show me his finished product.

Rather gruffly I insinuated that I wasn't all that impressed with his work. Perhaps I was just a little irked by the distraction in the hot sun, but I told him that the seal itself was not that complex, and you didn't need to be a seasoned sailor to work out how to replicate it. Rather, it was the *unsealing* of the knot which was most remarkable, when it was done.

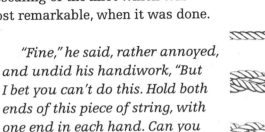

"Fine," he said, rather annoyed, and undid his handiwork, "But I bet you can't do this. Hold both ends of this piece of string, with one end in each hand. Can you tie it in a knot without letting go of either end?"

I told him I didn't have time for this kind of whimsical challenge, and could he copy out the hieroglyphs on this alabaster cup that his mentor and I were logging, please. He was rather disgruntled, but fortunately he did as he was told; I say fortunately, since I had absolutely no idea how it could be done.

Do you?

THE TOUR

The artefacts I painstakingly retrieve from tombs are generally destined for museums, where they might be enjoyed and admired by their patrons, who in turn become captivated with their mystique which in turn creates a yearning for yet more such artefacts.

It is my hope that my discoveries will one day tour the world so that they might be seen by as many people as possible, and the riches of this ancient civilization become known to all. I wonder if those ancient kings could ever have dreamed of the places their possessions might travel, long after their passing, or perhaps their journey with them into the afterlife was all that concerned them.

I have been fortunate to travel far and wide in this profession, in a way few get to do, although it is easy to miss the comforts of home. By contrast with my footslog, there is a particular object which frequently journeys to all four corners of the earth, and yet never leaves the corner it is most firmly stuck in.

What unlikely voyager is this?

A WHOLE NEW PROBLEM

One day, as we brushed away the sands of time and recovered marvellous objects, a colleague turned to me with the wry smile that I knew preceded a joke or riddle, and said:

> *"Today we are making our own collection bigger by taking away artefacts, but what is it that gets bigger itself the more you take away from it?"*

The answer came to me immediately, and I must admit I felt that the solution seemed rather obvious. But there were others on the dig who found it most puzzling, so I thought it worth mentioning.

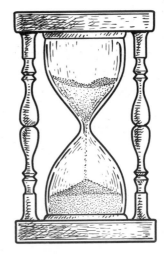

What was he referring to?

ORDERLY

My notebooks are precious items; within them, I have logged hundreds of items, registered a hundred hieroglyphs, and quietly recorded diverse aspects of a distant past. Of my more significant findings, of course, there are copies made, and the artefacts often speak for themselves, but I am sure to keep my personal notes safe, in case I should need them in the future.

To my great disappointment, a book used for notation several years ago has recently come to some damage, having had a pail of water accidentally spilled over it at an excavation site. I had been referring to the book to help me with the day's work, for the tomb we had discovered bore some resemblance to one I had unveiled many years ago, and I wanted to look upon my notes again and compare the findings.

The page I most needed was, alas, water-damaged, and the ink so smudged that it made much of the writing illegible. Back then, we had discovered three chambers in a tomb, with one person lain to rest in

each: according to their cartouches we had discovered a king, a queen, and a prince. The three tombs were of different sizes and inscriptions found in the chambers told us that the three had been buried at different times. From the remainders of my notes, however, only the following information was discernible:

- **The king was not interred first**

- **The person interred in the largest chamber was not the queen**

- **The prince was buried in the mid-size chamber**

- **The person interred second was buried in the smallest chamber**

I needed to work out who had been buried last, and in what size chamber, to help me with the most recent discovery. Can you tell from my disfigured notes which royal mummy was found in each tomb, and in what order they had been placed there?

PAPYRUS AND PAILS

Some tombs are immaculately organized, with the owner's possessions—and inner organs—neatly lined up within as though ready for inspection. Others are a little more ramshackle, perhaps after an unfortunate encounter with a graverobber, and have an appearance more like a jumble sale than a royal shrine. Of course, some of these underground chambers were intended as caches, so one never knows what might be waiting within—but it's part of the appeal of the work.

In those more disorganized crypts, some seem to have been sealed in a hurry, with unlikely objects left behind for some historian to wonder over in the future. I excavated one such tomb last year and I remember, near the entrance, I came across a scrap of papyrus next to what appeared to be two empty water pails, which were all three in very poor condition.

A few words were visible on the ancient paper, but most of the writing—and sense—was obscured. Near the top of the papyrus were a few clear hieroglyphs, however. They said:

Two pails: one will hold exactly eight units when full, and the other exactly five units when full.

Draw water from the Nile.

The boy king requires exactly six units of water.

Measure them precisely, using the method as follows...

But the hieroglyphs below were muddled, the ink faded and blurred, and their meaning lost. I looked back at the pails, no longer watertight, and wondered how they might have looked all those years ago, drawing water from the great Nile. It seemed strange that they had been left here, apparently in a hurry, frozen in time without perhaps ever having carried out the instructions on the papyrus.

But more importantly, I wondered, how could someone have used these two pails to measure out exactly six units worth of water from the river, without guessing, or using any other equipment?

THE HIEROGLYPHIC PYRAMID

At the entrance to an outer tomb I noticed a series of scratches on the wall. For several days I paid them scant attention and walked on past, assuming they had been caused by a delinquent cat, that animal so beloved of the ancient residents of this land.

But then, on a day that had hitherto been filled with a frustrating lack of progress, I discerned that there did in fact seem to be some kind of pattern to them.

In fact, I had been quite wrong. What was scratched on the wall transpired to be a coded number sequence, written in ancient hieroglyphs. It had been created in the shape of a pyramid, which was bemusingly apt, and with the sequence increasing in number of scratches at each stage as the marks descended down the face of the pyramid.

The final line of the sequence, however, had been erased by apparent flood damage, washed into historical oblivion by the annual flood of the Nile.

I carefully transcribed the scratched hieroglyphs into my pad, as follows:

Can you deduce, as I eventually did, how the final line must once have read?

ONE MAN'S TREASURE...

I have just returned from an arduous afternoon's work in the hot sun and, far from being fruitful, the latest excavations are turning up far too little. Indeed the only excitement was when one of our team proclaimed to have found something in their corner of the dig.

They described it thus:

> *"Well it's certainly a curio. There's a neck here—but no head, which is rather rare. And two long arms are here but, look—no hands at all."*

I couldn't get a good look at the object as the others gathered round, and the description certainly didn't help to clear things up. I wondered if he might be describing some depiction of a demi-god, but then even the part-animal deities had heads of some kind.

Upon closer inspection, however, it did not seem to be a hugely significant artefact. In fact, I don't believe it was from an ancient civilization at all, as I have never seen such an item depicted on the murals or scrolls in the tombs and temples. It was, all in all, a rather mundane find.

Can you discern what it was, based on the vague clues of my colleague?

INSIDE AND OUTSIDE

One particularly hot morning, I was joined on the excavation of a tomb by a young academic whose passion lay in ancient agriculture. She was, in a monologue, explaining the subject of a recent study of hers, and despite her loquacity she eventually made the following remarks:

> *"It is a curious thing for sure, although it never lived alongside the pharaohs. A most unusual foodstuff, where the outside is peeled and the inside is cooked—but then the outside is eaten, and the inside thrown away."*

No wonder the ancient Egyptians didn't bother with this particular edible, I thought to myself. There didn't seem to be much point in continuing the story, so I asked her to focus on the work right in front of us, as the day was hot, and I weary.

I never did take the time to puzzle out what matter she might have been talking about, but perhaps you will have more luck. Can you ascertain the subject of my fellow scholar's study?

A WORTHY WINNER

The fragments of text which survive from ancient worlds can give us only an idea of the full and multi-faceted lives lived by those who came before us. Indeed, those words which have endured the tests of time are generally those which have been deliberately preserved, bearing witness to an important political decree or perhaps a sacred scripture of some kind. It is altogether more curious, I find, to discover those scraps of paper and papyrus which tell us of the ordinary lives of any ancient people; of how they truly lived from day to day. Not worthy of murals, perhaps, but captivating nonetheless.

I recall once translating a work which detailed an amusing dispute between two siblings that had arisen during some sort of sporting event. Why on earth this was significant enough to be committed to eternity I cannot say, but it obviously had provoked some strong feelings at the time. There appeared to have been a running race with several participants, and the rule was simple: whoever ran the fastest and crossed the finishing line first would be the winner. The siblings— an older brother and his younger sister—had been part of the cohort taking part.

The brother was fast, and frequently ran ahead of his sister. He ran in second place for almost the whole race, until, just as he approached the finish line, his sister overtook him—crassly celebrating her victory as she crossed over the line. The brother immediately protested, according to the writings, and claimed that the triumph was completely unfair. The younger sister, it seemed, had been given a head start at the beginning of the race, and now the brother was arguing that if the advantage had not been given to start with, then *he* would have been the winner. The head start, apparently, was much bigger that the margin by which she overlapped him at the end. The brother protested that, in retrospect, he had been cheated and should be recognized as the true winner of the race.

I was most amused by the recording of the event, and noted the ingenious solution which had been supplied to the two siblings when they both appealed that they had won. Whoever was giving judgement on this conundrum was absolutely unequivocal about who the winner was.

Who do *you* think had won the race?

BRICK BY BRICK

I work predominantly in the Valley of the Kings, but I have seen a few of the pyramids at Giza which seem to capture the attention of so many readers at home. A tomb is a tomb, with an underground crypt being quite commonplace the world over, but a pyramid is quite unlike anything that I have ever seen. Indeed, we are still none the wiser about how these magnificently designed edifices were put together, so it is only natural that they inspire a certain fascination.

I remember the first time I gazed upon them, these pyramids I had heard so much about, and marvelled at their sheer size. The largest of the three most notable structures reaches over a hundred metres in height, towering over the necropolis, and for a few thousand years it was the tallest construction in the world. I found myself quietly wondering, as I looked upon the four faces of this impossible assembly: how many stone bricks does it take to complete a structure like that? Ten thousand? More?

Ancient measurements have been discovered on papyrus, the stones measured in palms and digits. The Great Pyramid itself must have reached some 280 Egyptian royal cubits in height, with the bases having

a length of 440 or so cubits, which in turn seems to be around 230 metres, in our most modern units. The individual stones themselves were rather large, perhaps 2 cubits by 2 cubits. Quite magnificent.

As I have grown older, and gained more experience in the architecture of such complex constructions, I have had the time to think of a more certain answer to a specific question. But perhaps you'll take a little less time to calculate a response.

How many bricks do you think were used to complete the largest pyramid at Giza?

MODERN CHARIOTS

It is quite a luxury to be transported around the sites of antiquity by automobile.

I remember being driven to an excavation site some years ago and, at the exact moment I arrived, an antiquated chariot was being brought out of the tomb. I marvelled at the juxtaposition of the old and the new, the chariot and the car, and thought once more of just how much time had passed between the sealing of these tombs and their unsealing by us.

I was lost in thought as I alighted from the car and so, it appears, was our driver. Having failed to apply the brakes, the car began to roll forward at pace and eventually came to a stop beneath a stone canopy, with the bonnet of the car wedged below the low lintel of the flat stone arch.

We pushed and pulled to try and release the automobile, everyone lending their own strength to the task. Alas, it would not move an inch, neither forward nor backward. It was, by all accounts, completely stuck.

Fortunately, a sharp-witted apprentice thought of something which he was sure would ensure the release of the car.

What do you think he suggested?

A DISAPPOINTING DISCOVERY

The road to success is paved with red herrings, and more than once has an excavation been plagued with false hope and spurious discoveries.

Just this morning, indeed, as I was unpacking a tomb with an experienced team, an assistant lifted a sack into the air and waved to bring it to my attention, that I might comment on its contents. I could not discern what might be in it from the distance at which he stood, but my colleague felt it was sure to contain something which might pique my interest. He moved over to where I stood, so I might look inside.

To my dissatisfaction, it *did* have something in it, but that something was such that it meant that, in fact, there was nothing in it at all.

What did I see?

THE CREATURE

Often, on a dig, we will have to set up some kind of temporary accommodation on site, usually consisting of some elaborately-constructed tents which fortunately I am not required to assist with assembling. It is a strange thing, to rest your head after a hot day's work with only a thin canvas sheet separating you from the stars and the sudden chill which descends when the sun sets over the sand. On these nights, I find I have the most absurd dreams; vivid conversations with the gods and kings I might have come across in stories in the daylight hours, etched into the walls of other, more permanent resting places.

I recall that I awoke in such a camp one morning, many years ago, to find that a fellow excavator in the adjacent tent appeared to have had some peculiar vision, not unlike a vivid dream, in the middle of the night. He tried his best to grapple verbally with what he had seen, describing some sort of ethereal creature in the vaguest and least helpful terms imaginable.

"It was a cat, you see—exactly the size and shape of a cat—but when I reached out to touch it, I couldn't grab hold of it at all. But there it was,

still, in the walls of my tent, although leaving no pawprints behind on my furnishings. Spectral. It was quite unreal. And yet, real."

"Are you quite sure, compadre, that you didn't dream up this creature?" I said, feeling rather tired and nonplussed myself, in the early morning sun.

"Oh, no," said he, "I saw it in my tent. Make no mistake."

I did not wish to insult my learned friend, so I didn't push any further. Privately, I had come up with my own theory of what he might have seen from his tent that night, and realized that it was neither spectral nor a dream.

What do you think it was?

THE FAST

Long ago, in my early career, I worked within the walls of an ancient temple, and had the pleasure of revealing a mural which detailed a most unusual story. It was the tale of a man whose piety was unmatched, and whose life had been painted out as an example to others of how one might choose to live a virtuous life. It was a joy to delicately brush away dust and dirt, and unravel the chronicle of the past, bringing it almost to life, reading the extraordinary story as we cleaned.

In one particular passage the man, in order to show his commitment to the gods, did not eat or drink for forty consecutive days. He was rewarded with a long life, and lived another forty years after his fast.

It was a rather inspiring tale, and certainly had been painted exquisitely on the walls of the temple—although a rather unlikely one too, I thought. Indeed, how could a man survive without divine intervention, if he did not eat a morsel, nor drink a drop, for forty days in a row?

But then I did think of a solution. What was it?

OF THE REIGNS
OF KINGS

When I return to London, I find that all those I encounter are fascinated by the now legendary excavations I have engaged in, and of course none more so than that of the boy king of the 18th dynasty.

Sometimes I set riddles for the youngest of my admirers, so they can partake in the thrill of discovery we all feel when these monumental steps forward in our historical understanding are made.

On occasions I pose them the following riddle:

"Tutankhamun was born many years ago, in the year 1344. He then died at the age of nineteen, in 1325. How can this be?"

How indeed?

THE WATER CLOCK

In my earliest days as an excavator's aide, I was charged with logging a magnificent water clock which we had discovered in what appeared to be perfect working order. The design is similar to an hourglass, where a certain amount of water is poured into the open top of the clock and allowed to drip out at the bottom at a steady rate, its passage thus marking a pre-determined amount of time. It is a rather ingenious piece of work and this particular item was most beautiful, etched with hieroglyphs on the outside and chronological measurements within.

Outside the tomb, my mentor challenged me over a lunch break to create a water clock just like the one I had been logging—after all, what we had found was not a toy but an artefact, and we were not at liberty to fill it with water ourselves and test it. I had copied out its design very carefully and so felt confident that I could construct something similar in function, if not decoration. The next morning, before we entered the tomb again, I presented my mentor with what I considered to be a perfect working replica of the water clock we had found, noting that it should measure out exactly three hours of time.

"Perfect," replied my mentor, who was preparing to enter the tomb, "Set up your clock, and begin the timer. In two hours we'll break for a while, and then there ought to be an hour left on your water clock, if you have made it well. What do you think?"

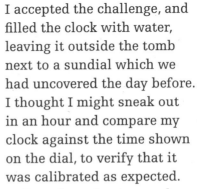

I accepted the challenge, and filled the clock with water, leaving it outside the tomb next to a sundial which we had uncovered the day before. I thought I might sneak out in an hour and compare my clock against the time shown on the dial, to verify that it was calibrated as expected.

In an hour, however, when I came to check on my water clock, it was quite impossible to tell the time with it for it was already empty. Alas, I realized all too late the flaw in my logic, and wondered how on earth I could have been so short-sighted.

Why do you think the clock had not worked?

BACK TO
RECTANGLE ONE

I once had the pleasure of uncovering, alongside an esteemed collaborator, a most unusual tiled floor in an ancient temple. The placement of the stones had been manipulated to form a rather curious pattern and, along with my co-excavator, I set about trying to determine how the floor had been pieced together.

Unfortunately, my colleague and I were not quite in agreement about how many pieces of stone might have been used to create the floor in the first place. Nature and wear seemed to have caused cracks to appear in some of the tiles, making surprisingly straight lines along the grain, and which made it tricky to see the size, shape, and quantity of the original tiles. The floor, when I had sketched it out with all the unfortunate fractures, looked like the image at the top of the opposite page.

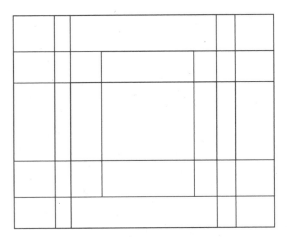

My fellow archaeologist believed the floor had been made of a few, large rectangular pieces of stone, which time had broken up into these smaller tiles. I personally argued that the stones had been broken up into smaller tiles by the architects, and then laid down as we saw them. Either way, neither of us could definitively determine which joins were intentional, and which were not. Indeed, based on the shapes we could see before us there seemed to have been a huge number of possible combinations of tiles laid down. My colleague thought 100, but I counted many more than that.

How many rectangles and squares can you make from the floor pattern, in total? Include shapes of all size, including the large rectangle all around the outside.

SOCIAL NICETIES

L ast week I attended a function at a museum of antiquities, where patrons and fellow archaeologists were encouraged to get acquainted, swap stories, and perhaps make large donations to the museum. I had no intention of undertaking any of these tasks, but my own benefactor was attending and I was compelled to attend with him.

Unfortunately, I soon discovered my scepticism was well-founded, for the host had prepared an activity for the guests, with participation obligatory. He said:

> *"To help us become better acquainted, I propose that you each move about the room, introducing yourselves and your work to one another—but, to make it more interesting, that you should only shake hands with anyone who has journeyed to more countries than you."*

There were some rather competitive types in the group, and I loathe this sort of exercise, so I slipped out of the room for a moment pretending to be in search of a drink, that I might avoid this enforced frivolity altogether.

It also then occurred to me that, of the thirty-four people in the room, I already knew exactly how many handshakes would take place. How many indeed?

WEEP AND WORSHIP

Many years ago, I heard of a most unusual offering that was frequently made to Egyptian pharaohs. This object was revered since it was hoped that it might bring its bearers eternal life, and was often buried alongside those members of society who had hoped for immortality.

I once uncovered some apparent remains of this particular object, which was found in a box inscribed rather helpfully with a description of how it came to be placed there, deep in a tomb. The text did rather appear to describe a harrowing end, since the label translated more or less as follows:

> *"The skin was cut and peeled back, and it made the people weep; but it did not weep for itself, and then it was entombed."*

What had joined this long-ago pharaoh in their hoped-for journey to the afterlife?

TROUBLE BREWING

Household drama, it seems, has no age. The history books are full of in-fighting between relatives and it seems that the ancient Egyptians were no different. On a scroll of papyrus I was recently tasked with transliterating, I uncovered one such spectacle concerning a family of brewers and the division of a fermented legacy.

The head brewer was the family's matriarch, and wanted her three daughters to join her in the malting business. She had at the time been in the process of making beer to sell, and had fifteen vessels in her workshop: five were full, five half-full, and five empty.

She told the sisters to divide the vessels fairly and exactly among themselves so they each had the same number of full, half-full, and empty vessels, without using any kind of measuring device. Once they had divided them equally, they could take their quantities out and sell them, and keep whatever they earned. Naturally, she forbade them from disposing of any of the beer, but she consented that they could move beer between vessels if they wished.

The vessels were all held the same amount of beer, but were all rather irregular in shape, so it would be impossible to merely see by eye when a vessel was half-full, and unhelpfully they were not labelled in any way. Protesting, therefore, that it could not be done, the sisters fought: the youngest thought she should have all the full ones while the older girls made more beer, while the oldest felt that she alone was deserving of the fullest vessels. The head brewer, however, was unswayed, and told the girls they would be able to divide the beer and vessels fairly, as she had described.

Fortunately, this aged piece of writing also detailed how the girls eventually came to their solution, as I could not for the life of me work out how they might have done it. Can you?

THE AMULETS

This morning I had the pleasure of logging the contents of an antechamber, in the small tomb of a young nobleman whose identity was rather obscure. There were the usual trappings of a well-preserved burial place, and the walls were rather ornately decorated with scenes from the *Book of the Dead*. Clearly this inhabitant was a keen would-be resident of the ancient Egyptian afterlife.

Unfortunately, I was joined by a rather clumsy colleague during the excavation who, not looking where he was going, disturbed an arrangement of amulets I had been logging, and indeed had been about to photograph. There had been ten scarab amulets arranged in a triangular formation—perhaps harking to some mystic ritual of which I had no knowledge—and I had been hoping to capture them exactly as I found them, in case there was any significance in their precise positioning. Hurriedly, he picked up the scarabs which had been jostled and placed them back into what he thought was their original set-up, so that it looked something like that shown below:

Alas, my unhandy colleague was quite mistaken in his placement—the triangle shape I had originally found was pointing down towards me, rather than up, as he had arranged them. I was keen that the priceless artefacts be touched by as few hands as possible, however, and so I hurried to recreate the correct arrangement by moving only three scarabs. As a result, the triangle could be restored to its original orientation, pointing straight at me.

How could I do it by touching just three scarabs?

RISING WATER

An apprentice once joined me on a six-day boat trip up the Nile. He claimed he had come up with an ingenious method of fishing that meant he could study our work closely on deck, while fishing in the ancient style on the river without compromising either project.

He tied and hung his line, hook, and bait off the side of the boat very carefully, so that the bait was exactly 2 feet above the surface of the river. The river, he knew, would rise 1/2 a foot—6 inches, that is—every day during our trip, due to the season, and his plan was simply to wait until the bait was submerged and he would be able to catch a fish without ever having to pay attention to the line. Time would do the work for him.

Given how long his line was, how many days do you think it took for the bait to enter the water, and how soon, therefore, might he hope to catch a fish?

NATURAL PHENOMENON

I recently read through a translated passage which detailed some salient weather events of its time, chronicling floods and droughts, sandstorms, and even rainstorms.

Rain being somewhat scarcer in ancient Egypt than in England, there was one particular detail which surprised me in the passage. According to this almanac, rain had recently passed through the land bringing a most unusual object with it, from the point of view of those long-ago inhabitants. Indeed it was something which, no matter how long it stood out in the anomalous rainstorm, could never get any wetter. And yet later it disappeared without a trace.

What was it that caused such perplexity?

THE PLOUGH

It is quite a marvel to me that the ancient Egyptians, unable to tame the mighty Nile, still made the most of the fertile riches it brought them each year with their extensive irrigation systems. The flooding—and its resulting silt—left fantastically fertile land behind for them to till and grow their produce.

Not everyone seems to have benefitted from the agricultural marvel, however. On a recent excavation I uncovered a mural detailing a rather unfortunate exchange between a farmer and his farmhand, a young boy. It was painted quite splendidly upon a wall, with the blue of the omnipresent Nile just visible in the background.

The farmer told the boy to take the oxen out onto a field, and plough the whole thing to turn all the soil. He would pay him for his work at the end of the day, depending on how much of it he had managed to plough.

The boy went out, drove the oxen, and came back when the sun set. To his dismay, the farmer had not yet calculated what was owed to him and, instead, he wanted the boy to do it.

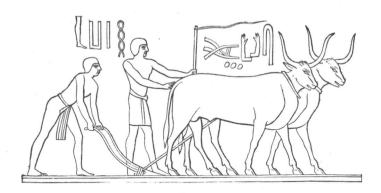

"Go out," he said, "And count the number of steps taken by your oxen. I will give you one ear of emmer for each step they took".

This seemed fair to the boy, who thought that he himself must have taken a hundred steps to walk one length of the field, and he must have done that fifty or so times. He was going to be due quite an embarrassment of riches, by his estimation; but being fair, he went back into the field to count the number exactly. Out he went, and saw how many hoofprints had been left behind by his beasts of burden.

The boy returned to the farmer as the light was fading fast, and told him what he had counted.

How many ears of emmer do you think the farmer gave the young boy?

LOOTED LOOT

Looters, fakes and tricksters are an unfortunate but apparently ubiquitous blemish on the business of archaeology. As an archaeologist and expert on antiquities, it is merely my office to guide artefacts to their new homes in museums and galleries, that they might be preserved for several more centuries to come. Alas, not everyone regards priceless finds in the same way.

I was leaving an office of antiquities last night when I was approached by a person who claimed they had something to show me. He did, indeed, have a small tray with four gold discs on it which looked rather genuine to me—so genuine, in fact, that I became quite suspicious as to how this gentleman had come to be in possession of them. I asked him tactfully who they belonged to.

> "Oh, you, Sir," he replied bizarrely, before continuing, "If you just solve a little puzzle of mine, you can have these priceless treasures. But if you try and fail, I'll ask you to give me one of your treasures."

I didn't want to fall into any trap, but I did want to know what this person's business was, so I waited mutely for him to continue.

"These four discs aren't arranged as I found them. When I found them, they were in two straight rows, with three discs in each row."

I looked at the four discs he had in his little tray, which were arranged as below, and rather wondered if he had lost his mind when he found this treasure:

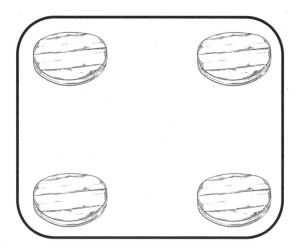

"I'll let you pick up one disc—just one—to see if you can recreate the two rows just as I found them. If you do, they're yours."

I didn't make an attempt at his challenge—not wanting to negotiate with a possible graverobber—but I did see how it could be done. Do you?

AN URN-EST PROBLEM

There are many minor tombs in the Valley of the Kings, and one day I happened upon a relatively undisturbed burial chamber that contained the sarcophagus of some unnoted member of an ancient royal household.

Laid out within the tomb were nine ancient urns, arranged as follows:

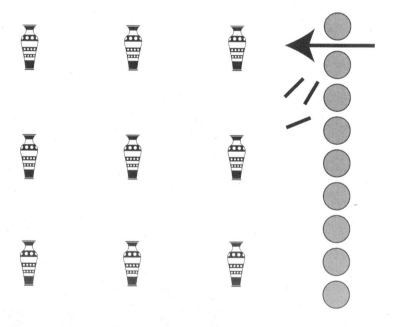

Near them were the remains of three reflective plates that I took to have been used as primitive mirrors. They would once have been arranged in such a way that all of the urns could have been illuminated via just one single narrow beam of light, which I discerned would in long ago times have shone in from a burning candle placed behind a pair of columns.

I have marked the direction of the narrow beam of light on the picture of the urns opposite. Can you work out where the plates should be placed so that this one beam of light will illuminate all nine urns? Assume that the beam of light passes over the tops of the urns so they do not themselves impede the flow of light, and that the plates are tall enough that the urns do not interfere with them.

THE LONGEST RIVER

I once had an apprentice who was not what you might consider the sharpest pointing trowel in the archaeologist's bag. He was the boy with whom I journeyed on the Nile and who attempted to fish by a somewhat rudimentary—and indeed fundamentally flawed—method.

On that same boat trip, I was telling him a little more about the Nile, wondering that its true source had remained unknown for many centuries, being, as it was, the longest river in all of that great continent of Africa. Indeed, the river was once believed to have sprung from a mythical mountain range some way south of us: the Mountains of the Moon.

It was only when more recent explorers ventured to the great lakes that we eventually revealed its true beginnings—and the true length—of the immense river which we cruised along.

The young boy took particular interest in this revelation, asking "So what was the longest river in Africa, before the length of the Nile was discovered?"

What answer did I give?

PAINTED PHARAOHS

Just after we broke for lunch one day, at a conference I was attending back in London, I heard an "amusing" acquaintance of mine regale his devotees there with the following question:

> *"When we discover these incredible ancient murals, do you know why it is that we never record paintings of pharaohs with photographic cameras?"*

I heard much murmuring of answers, such as that perhaps they were too impractical to take to distant and dusty places.

But I had heard this before, and knew the "comedic" answer he intended.

Can you guess what it was?

SNAKING SOLUTION

Sometimes during the course of our archaeological expeditions we have cause to make minor restoration to areas we excavate, to ensure the preservation of material too delicate to survive for long when exposed to our modern air.

On several occasions we have uncovered the most delicate of snake reliefs, where the body of an asp had been threaded most intricately around a number of tiny pins. This ancient thread was now long gone, but by luck the artists of old had labelled the number of pins that the thread visited in each row and column.

The remains of the head and tail of the snake were marked on the relief, as shown below—and for your convenience I have also converted the hieroglyphic numbers into Arabic numerals.

Can you draw a thread that runs from the head to the tail, visiting the exact number of pins shown in each row and column? For historical accuracy ensure that the thread does not cross over any of the solid pieces of stone, indicated with grey squares, nor travel diagonally at any point.

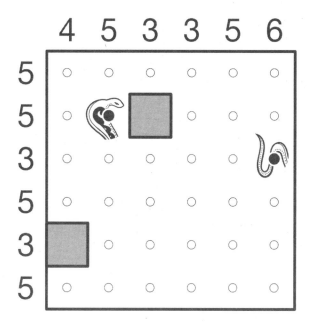

HEAVEN AND EARTH

I make no secret of my joy in discovering now-seemingly mundane objects and entities which were once revered by ancient cultures; that were once held up as a marvellous gift from the gods, to be worshipped and exalted accordingly.

Indeed, I was once told of a certain being that was highly favoured by the pharaoh Cleopatra, as it manifested some divine qualities. It had no shoulders, or arms, or hands—and indeed no legs or feet at all—and yet all day long it pushed and shoved the earth as it spun around on its axis. And, quite immaculately, it had no eyes to see *where* it was moving the earth to.

I suppose it was the unlikeliness of this ostensibly ill-equipped creature being able to move the earth that captured the imagination.

But what was it that was so celebrated?

SOLUTIONS

P.8. THE CODE

- From the second statement, the egret can be positioned as the third image.
- The vase can be ruled out as an option from the final statement—because the only correct image is one place to the right of where it should be, the far-left image must be absent.
- This in turn rules the vase out of the first statement, meaning that the cat and the jackal must be the remaining two correct images. From this, the beetle, eye and bull can be eliminated entirely.
- In the first statement we know that the cat is in the wrong position, since the egret is in the third position, which means that the jackal must be the symbol in the correct position.
- This then leaves the cat to go in the only remaining unsolved position, as the first symbol.

P.10. THE PARTY

Zero probability. Since she assigned all the names in advance, to be correct about the remaining twenty-four names then she would have had to have been correct about the first—or used a name more than once. We already know that none of the names were otherwise repeated.

P.12. THE SIBLINGS

Menna. In order from oldest to youngest, the siblings were Beket, Khamudi, Menna, Ahmose and Hor.

P.13. THE ORACLE

45. One fifth of 45 is 9, and 45+9=54—which is 45 in reverse.

P.14. THE AMULETS

Bastet is wearing the scarab amulet, Sobek is wearing the cat amulet, and Khepri is wearing the crocodile amulet.

Bastet cannot be wearing the crocodile amulet since we know she is replied to by the god who is wearing it, and she cannot be wearing a cat amulet as this is the animal she embodies. Therefore, Bastet must be wearing the scarab. This in turn means that Khepri must be wearing the crocodile amulet and Sobek is wearing the cat amulet.

P.16. THE LOCKED TOMB

I would need to acquire three padlocks and cut two keys for each.

Say that the padlocks were labelled 1, 2, and 3, and the archaeologists A, B, and C. I would need to give person A the keys to 1 and 2, person B the keys to 2 and 3, and person C the keys to 1 and 3. This would mean that everyone could enter the tomb, but only as part of a pair, since between them they would always have the keys to all three padlocks, but on their own this would never be the case.

P.18. THE REFRESHMENT TENT

Pick up the first and third cups and pour the water from them into the sixth and eighth cups, replacing them in their original positions.

P.20. THE FADED SCROLL

One in three. Disregarding for a moment the fact that we know at least one child is a boy, there are four possible situations for the combination of sexes in the two children:

1. Both children are girls
2. The first child is a girl and the second child is a boy
3. The first child is a boy and the second child is a girl
4. Both children are boys

If we did not know the sex of either of the children, the chance of both being boys would be one in four. However, because we know that at least one is a boy, the first option in the list can be eliminated. This leaves three options featuring at least one boy, one of which is that both children are boys, giving a probability of one in three that both are boys.

P.21. SENET SERIES

We were playing different opponents. Once I clarified this to my colleague, it made sense to him. It later occurred to me that an alternative explanation would have been that the archaeologist and I had been playing together as a team.

P.22. THE EXCAVATORS

Seven—four sisters and three brothers. Any sister would have three sisters and three brothers, while any of the brothers would have four sisters and two brothers.

P.24. EVENING ENTERTAINMENT

Jan would first have to deal to himself, as the person who would have received the last card from the deck, but dealing up from the bottom of the pack. Continuing in an anti-clockwise direction he would then deal upwards from the bottom until all the cards had been dealt. In this way he would guarantee that each person received the exact cards they otherwise would have done had the deal not been interrupted.

P.26. THE QUESTION

The gold and silver figures are both lying, and the figure in green is telling the truth.

If the green figure is lying then both the gold and silver figures are, in fact, telling the truth. This would mean, however, that the gold figure is able to call the silver figure a liar, per the silver figure's statement, which would not be true. Given this contradiction, the green figure must instead be telling the truth, and therefore—as the green figure states—the gold and silver figures are liars.

P.28. COIN CLASSIFICATION

I should arrange the coins into the shape of a six-pointed star, with one coin at each point of the star and one coin at each point where the sides of the star intersect.

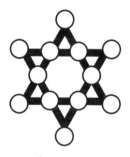

P.29. SCHEDULING THE DIG

I would need six archaeologists. If four archaeologists can excavate four blocks in four days, it takes one archaeologist four days to excavate one block. As a result, in twenty days, one archaeologist could do five blocks. To complete the excavation of the thirty blocks in the allocated time, I would therefore need six archaeologists.

P.30. ENTERING THE TOMB

One hour exactly. First, Mace and Lythgoe should climb together, taking ten minutes. Then, Lythgoe should return to the start of the tunnel with the lantern, taking a further ten minutes. Next, Burton and myself should cross together, taking twenty-five minutes. Mace should then go back with the lantern, taking five minutes. Mace and Lythgoe should then travel through together for a second time, taking ten minutes—and therefore sixty minutes in total. This would also work if Mace and Lythgoe swapped roles in this schedule.

P.32. THE SCHOLAR

Sneferu is the earliest, then the ordering is Khufu, Djedefre, Khafre, and finally Menkaure is the most recent.

P.34. THE GAME NIGHT

You would need to draw thirty-eight coins. With forty-two coins in the bag of six types, and an equal number of each, there must be $42 \div 6 = 7$ of each type of coin. So, to guarantee three of each coin, you must allow for drawing all of the coins of the first five types, and three of the sixth type, which is a total of $(5 \times 7) + 3 = 38$ coins. If you drew any fewer, there would be a possibility that you would not yet have three of every kind. But drawing any more would be unnecessary..

P.35. THE SCRIBE'S ACCOUNT

In the first family, the father had ground twenty-one bags, the mother twenty bags, the girl five bags and the boy four bags. In the second family, the father had ground nineteen bags, the mother fifteen bags, the girl ten bags and the boy six bags.

P.37. THE WATER BARREL

I suggested tilting the barrel until the water was just about to pour out of the top. If the barrel was over half full, the bottom of the barrel would remain submerged. If the barrel was under half-empty, some of the bottom would be visible.

P.38. THE NIGHTMARE

The tallest figure was the truth-teller, the middle-height figure was the occasional liar, and the smallest figure was the liar. If the middle-height figure is telling the truth then so is the tallest figure; or conversely if he is lying then so is the tallest figure. If they were both lying then the smallest figure would have to be the truth-teller, but this cannot be the case as a truth-teller would not claim to be an occasional liar. So both the tallest and middle-height figures are telling the truth. This means that the smallest figure is the person who always lies. Because the tallest figure unequivocally states that they are the truth-teller, and we know this to be a true statement, then this identifies them as the truth-teller and so the middle-height figure must be the occasional liar, who is telling the truth on this occasion.

P.40. THE COUNTERFEIT SCARAB

Two comparisons are all that is needed.

First, divide the nine scarabs into three equal piles of three amulets each. Compare two of these piles, and then if the result is that one is heavier than the other you know that the fake amulet is in the lighter pile. If the two piles are equal, you know that the fake amulet is in the pile which you haven't yet weighed. No matter the result, you have narrowed the fake amulet down to a set of precisely three amulets.

Next, take the pile of three that contains the fake amulet and split it into three individual amulets, and compare two of them on the balance. If they weigh the same, you know that the fake amulet is the one which is not on the scales. Or, if one of them is lighter, this is the fake amulet.

So no matter the outcome, you have identified the fake in just two uses of the balance.

P..43. LOOKING FOR DIRECTIONS

I knew that I had set out from Karnak, so I need only point the relevant branch of the signpost in the direction I had come from to orientate it correctly, providing me with all the information I needed to continue my journey.

P44. SITE DISPUTE

He should place a single green amulet in the first bag, and the other nineteen amulets in the second bag. If the bags were instead left as they were, with all of the green in one bag and all of the blue in the other, I would have a 50% chance of drawing a green or a blue amulet. But by rearranging so that one bag contains a single green amulet, I have a 100% chance of drawing a green amulet from the first bag and an approximately 47% chance of drawing a green amulet from the second bag, as there are nine green amulets out of the total of nineteen. This means that the total chance of drawing a green is the sum of the probabilities of a green amulet from each bag, with each bag having a 50% chance of being chosen by me: (50% x 1) + (50% x 9/19)—or approximately 74%.

P.46. THE COIN TOSS

Lord Carnarvon is incorrect. The three options he gives are not equally likely, since the final winning event of "heads" on the first toss actually encompasses two events: heads + tails, and heads + heads. Therefore the chance of winning is in fact three in four.

P.47. HISTORICAL SENET

Thutmose and Khay, with Thutmose being the victor.

The losers took it in turns to play, so each player at a minimum must have played at least ten games. We know Khay played ten games in total, so for this minimum number of games he must have skipped the first game and then played in every second match, which would involve losing every match. So we know he was the loser of every even-numbered game, so he was the loser of match eighteen.

Prehotep played the first fifteen games but must have lost every match after that since he only played eighteen in total, so from match fifteen onwards he only played odd-numbered games. So Thutmose must have been the winner of match eighteen.

P.48. ANCIENT LOVERS

Sabni planned to set out from his town immediately after the sentry had completed one of their checks. He would then cross the bridge as briskly as possible for just *under* five minutes, then start running back towards his *own* town. The sentry would be likely to assume that Sabni was running from the town on the opposite side of the river to the town he had actually just come from, and escort him "back" to Satiah's town, which is where he wanted to go.

P.50. THE TAX COLLECTORS

Two. At each bridge, one bag of grain would be taken but also one would be returned.

P.51. THE CATTLE COUNT

I had sorted the numbers according to how many letters each had when spelled out as a word:
   2, 6, 10: Three letters—two, six, and ten
   3, 7, 8: Five letters—three, seven, and eight
   11, 12, 20: Six letters—eleven, twelve, and twenty
   13, 14, 19: Eight letters—thirteen, fourteen, and nineteen

P.52. THE DIFFICULT ARCHAEOLOGISTS

The crucial first step is transporting Edwin and Percy across the river, since without them none of the people left behind will fall out. The boat can then return and pick up any two people, but once these two further people are transported across the river it must return Edwin and Percy

back to the original bank, before bringing over the person who has not yet crossed the river. Finally it can return empty, and pick up Edwin and Percy again to bring them to the far side.

P.54. THE CURSED DREAM

Wait until night has fallen, then walk along the corridor unharmed.

P.56. THE FLOOD

On the thirteenth day, given that it was doubling in volume every day.

P.57. MAGICAL NUMBERS

It has all ten digits (0-9) appearing in alphabetical order of their spellings as words.

P.58. THE SECURITY GUARDS

Hasina	20:00 – 02:00 and 06:00 – 12:00
Khalid	00:00 – 06:00 and 12:00 – 18:00
Anthony	08:00 – 14:00 and 18:00 – 00:00
Maat	02:00 – 08:00 and 14:00 – 20:00

P.60. LADY EVELYN'S NOTE

T, S and S. The sequence is the initial letters of each word from the final sentence of the note.

P.61. THE FRAGMENTS OF PAPYRUS

With each fragment used once, the names of the six objects can be assembled:

BANDAGE	CANOPIC JAR
AMULET	INCENSE
MASK	SARCOPHAGUS

P.62. A MATTER OF TIME

Eleven. All of the months of the year, bar February, have thirty days—or more specifically, *at least* thirty days. Needless to say I was quite unimpressed with his deliberate ambiguity.

P.64. VISION

A window.

P.66. MISCHIEVOUS TWINS

As the two statements given by the twins do not agree, at least one must be lying. Now if Baahir is telling the truth then the statement "neither of us are liars" must be true, which is not correct, so Baahir is definitely lying. From this it can be seen that Ammon is in fact telling the truth.

P.68. HIEROGLYPH FASCINATION

I had created the sets of letters according to whether straight or curved lines were used to draw the letters involved, or more specifically as to whether there were curves and/or corners in the letter. In particular the first set contained no curves, the second set contained curves but no corners, and the third set contained curves *and* corners. I had left out "Q" because I could not decide whether the angle from the line to the circle counted as a corner or not.

P.70. A NEW JUG

The jug was worth £3. With the flowers therefore worth £13, this gave the total price of £16.

P.71. ANOTHER NOTE FROM EVELYN

"Star". Each word can be preceded in sequence by a number to create a new, hyphenated adjective that can be found in a dictionary: "one-nation", "two-timing", "three-pronged", "four-poster". The only word of the given options which can be preceded by the word "five" (and thus continue the sequence) is "star", making "five-star" (as for example in "five-star general").

P.72. THE MARKET TRADER

He started by crossing with the duck, then crossed back over to collect one of the two remaining items—either the goat or the duck food. He then took this across the river but, crucially, when he then returned from the far side he brought back the duck with him to the original side. He then rowed to the far side with whichever was remaining of the goat or duck food, came back empty, picked up the duck and rowed once more to the opposite bank.

P.74. THE ARCHITECTS

He proposed to create a 3D structure with the reeds: a triangular-based pyramid. The four sides of the pyramid would form the four equally sized triangles.

P.76. DINNER WITH CARNARVON

He took each roll out of the basket one by one, broke it in half, and put one half of each roll onto each of our plates.

P.78. THE DIFFICULT JOURNEY

Yes, he would have saved time by walking all the way. By way of example, say that he walked at 4 mph. In this case, the car would have moved at 32 mph and the cart at 2 mph. Now say, by way of further example, that the entire journey was thirty-two miles. In such case the first half of the journey would have taken 30 minutes in the car, and the second half would have taken eight hours in the cart, giving a total journey time of eight hours thirty minutes. Conversely, walking at a steady 4 mph, he would have been able to cover the entire thirty-two miles in eight hours if he walked constantly for the whole distance, saving thirty minutes. And similarly for any other walking speed or distance, since these differences will scale proportionately.

P.79. DAILY DISTRACTION
Wednesday. Working backwards from the end of the puzzle, first note that two days after Friday would be Sunday. From here, you can calculate that Sunday's "tomorrow" is Monday, and for Monday to be considered "the day before yesterday", the speaker must be speaking on Wednesday.

P.80. A GAME OF HANDBALL
Hasani had started walking backwards as soon as Gamal had changed direction—so they had been facing each other, but had stayed about the same distance apart.

P.82. A LUNCH APPOINTMENT
The names of the locations are encoded using a letter-to-number cipher, with A being replaced by the number 1, B with 2, C with 3 and so on until Z is replaced with 26. In the order they appear, the decoded locations are therefore as follows:
HELIOPOLIS   SAQQARA
THEBES   ALEXANDRIA

P.84. STRANGE RELATIONS
The boy's father had married a much younger wife, whose own father (therefore being the boy's grandfather) was younger than that of her husband. Therefore the boy's father was older than the boy's mother's father.

P.85. A DIFFERENT KINGDOM
Three. The numbers after the words refer to the number of letters within each word which are part of the Roman numeral system: I, V, X, L, C, D or M. "VICTORY" has three Roman numeral letters, "V", "I", and "C", giving a solution of three.

P.86. A CLASSIFIED TASK
I would be the first to finish, on the ninth day.

If I doubled the number of artefacts I logged each day, I would reach 255 artefacts at the end of the eighth day (1+2+4+8+16+32+64+128). Smith would have logged 360 artefacts by this point (10+20+30+40+50+60+70+80). On the ninth day, Smith would log 90 further items, taking his total to 450, whereas I would log 256 further items, easily taking me past the total of 500.

P.87. AN UNFORTUNATE INCIDENT
Harry had dropped the necklace, and Abdel was telling the truth.

Alfred agrees with Hussein, so since we know that only one person is telling the truth then they must both by lying. Therefore Hussein must be lying, and Harry is also not telling the truth. As the only person left, Abdel must be telling the truth.

P.88. THE SPECIALISTS
Both Mary and Saleem make clear that they are not the Alexandrian literature specialist. As we know that this particular specialist is telling the truth, they indeed cannot have that speciality. That means that Albert must be the Alexandrian literature enthusiast, and that what he says is true: Saleem is the specialist in the

history of pyramid construction. This leaves Mary to be the Egyptian cuisine specialist.

P.90. THE CARRIAGE CLOCKS

Neither myself nor Callender has an advantage in this bet. I hypothesized that if I won the bet my winnings would be greater than the amount I stood to lose—but this was not true, since the value I stood to lose (the price of the more expensive clock) is the same as the amount I stood to win (also the value of the more expensive clock). So we are simply taking a 50:50 chance as to winning or losing.

P.92. THE BRUSHES

Four archaeologists and three brushes.

P.93. THE ARCHER

Twenty-one arrows, since he could preload the first one and fire it as the time began (i.e. at "0" seconds on a hypothetical clock), and fire the final one exactly as time ended. With three seconds for each reload, this would give a total of twenty-one arrows fired.

P.94. PHARAONIC NUMBERING

The numbers had been formed by adding together the number of letters in the name of each pharaoh along with the value represented by the Roman numeral following the name. For example, NEFERKARE has nine letters, which were added to the eight represented by VIII, to make seventeen.

P.96. THE BOASTFUL ARCHAEOLOGIST

The camel is speaking the truth. If the crocodile was speaking the truth, then the cobra's statement must also be true. As both animals cannot be telling the truth, we know that at least the crocodile is lying. If the cobra was speaking the truth, then the camel would also be speaking the truth. As again we know that only one of the animals is speaking the truth, it cannot either be the cobra. This means, by elimination, that it must be the camel.

P.98. THE FORGOTTEN NAME

His first initial was "O". Once I had worked this out, I immediately remembered that it stood for "Oscar".

P.99. THE BAKER

It was not a fair deal, since the customer would be getting less crispbread for his money. The area of a circular crispbread with a 4-inch diameter would be about 12.6 square inches, while a crispbread with an 8-inch diameter would have an area of about 50.3 square inches. Clearly, therefore two 4-inch crispbreads would still only give approximately half the crispbread of a single 8-inch item.

P.100. ORGANIZING THE VALLEY

Horus.

I realized that the KV number for each king showed me which letter to take from each line, ordered from left to right. This gave me 'S' for the first line, as it is the fourth letter in the row, since the tomb number is KV4. The hint about ordering the kings told me that, once extracted, the letters needed to be read in order of the reign of the rulers, which therefore started with the letter next to Rameses II and ended with the letter next to Rameses

XI. Following this system reveals 'HORUS', the Egyptian god who was believed to protect the monarchy.

P.101. THE BOOKSHELF
514 pages—one page of volume one, all 512 pages of volume two, and one page of volume three. This is because the first page of volume one is on the right as you look at it on the shelf, and the last page of volume three is on the left as you look at it.

P.102. THE GRANDFATHER CLOCK
Seven sets. For this, I would hear seven single chimes, which would involve waiting for up to just under an hour and three quarters, between just after 12:00 and until 1:45. In such a scenario, I would hear a single chime at 12.15, then another at 12.30, and so on until at 1:45 I heard a seventh single chime. Once I had heard the seventh single chime in a row, I would know that the time must be 1.45, and the bell would next chime twice, for 2.00. Until that point, however, I could not be sure from a shorter series of single chimes of the exact time.

P.104. THE SUPERVISOR
18, 31, and 32. Each printed, folded sheet has two pairs of consecutive numbers: the first has 1/2 and 47/48, the second has 3/4 and 45/46, and so on. Pairing up the numbers in this way, 17 and 18 are printed on the back of one another, and share a sheet with pages 31 and 32. So if page 17 was missing, the others must be too.

P.106. THE DATES
The first worker started with ten dates, while the second worker had twenty dates.

P.107. BURIED ALIVE
Plants and planting. Their seeds are buried in the earth before they become alive, and then are often only dug up again once they have died. They are also often transplanted into the ground while alive.

P.108. FRACTIONS OF EGYPT
100.
The easiest way to solve the problem is to start at the end and work backwards. Work out that nine tenths of one thousand is 900, and then that eight ninths of 900 is 800, seven eighths of 800 is 700, and so on and so on, until you reach 200 as two thirds of 300. Half of 200 is then 100, giving you your answer.

P.109. A TIME-CONSUMING CONUNDRUM
Some item of cutlery or crockery—which of course one buys in order to eat, but never actually eats.

P.110. THE THEBAN SENTRY
Because the sentry had evidently been asleep on his night duty—otherwise he would not have just had the long dream!

P.112. THE LINE OF SUCCESSION
Tiye is the mother of Satiah, who is the mother of Iaret, who is the mother of Amenia.

P.113. THE LIBRARY
The man was blind, and the book he was reading was a Braille book.

P.114. A PARTY AT HIGHCLERE
Seven people. This is possible because for example a single person could conceivably be all of a mother, grandmother, daughter, child, grandchild and sister,

although to be both grandmother and granddaughter would be somewhat unlikely!

In fact, it is possible to assign all of the relationships to just seven people as follows, numbering those people from 1 to 7 for ease of reference:

Person 1: Grandfather of 5, 6 and 7; father of 3; father-in-law of 4; husband of 2

Person 2: Grandmother of 5, 6 and 7; mother of 3; mother-in-law of 4; wife of 1

Person 3: Mother of 5, 6 and 7; child of 1 and 2; daughter of 1 and 2; wife of 4

Person 4: Father of 5, 6 and 7; son-in-law of 1 and 2; husband of 3

Person 5: Child of 3 and 4; son of 3 and 4; grandchild of 1 and 2; brother of 6 and 7

Person 6: Child of 3 and 4; son of 3 and 4; grandchild of 1 and 2; brother of 5 and 7

Person 7: Child of 3 and 4; son of 3 and 4; grandchild of 1 and 2; sister of 5 and 6

P.115. MISCHIEVOUS TWINS 2

Ammon was telling the truth, and the conversation took place on Thursday.

If Baahir was telling the truth, it would have had to be Sunday—the only day he can tell the truth about having been lying the day before. However, if it had indeed been Sunday then Ammon would have had to tell the truth too, but since he had *not* been lying the day before then he would have had to lie—which he was not allowed to do on Sunday. Assuming the twins are sticking to their rules, therefore, it must by elimination be Ammon telling the truth. And, for Ammon to have lied yesterday but be telling the truth today, it must be the only truth-telling day that immediately follows a lie-telling day, which means it is Thursday.

P.116. THE DREAM

If the man had died before waking up from this dream, there would have been no way for the details of the dream to be recounted.

P.118. FAMILY TREES

The sister is the writer's mother. If the writer's aunt had a sister who was not another aunt to her, then it must have been her mother.

P.120. DISTRACTION TECHNIQUES

Any of these solutions fits the requirements of the puzzle:

192, 384, 576
219, 438, 657
273, 546, 819
327, 654, 981

P.121. THE PUBLISHER

Nineteen letters: E, E, E, F, G, H, I, L, N, N, O, R, S, T, T, U, V, W, and X.

P.122. STONE RIDDLES

A shadow—which needs light to exist, but will disappear if you shine a light directly at it.

P.124. OUT OF DEPTH

Halfway. After that, one must be wading *out* again—although of course you'll end up on the other side of the river.

P.126. THE JOURNAL

The 31st January was on a Monday that year. To have only four Tuesdays and four Fridays, the month must have started on a Saturday, which would make the 31st a Monday.

P.127. THE SHATTERED BOX

Twenty-five of them—all of them apart from the cube from the very middle of the shape and the cube in the centre of the top side.

P.128. THE SOUND OF SILENCE

An echo. There are plenty of these to be found in the catacombs.

P.130. DUNG BEETLES

There is a three in four chance that there will be a collision. All three of the beetles would need to decide to travel either clockwise or anticlockwise to avoid a collision.

If the first beetle decides to travel clockwise, the chance that the second two beetles will follow suit is ½ x ½ = ¼, leaving a ¾ chance of them not all choosing the same direction—and therefore colliding.

P.131. THE FRESH-FACED ASSISTANT

The man was twenty-seven years old: 2 + 7 = 9, and 9 × 3 = 27.

P.132. THE FALL

Rain—which falls from clouds miles above our heads, and yet cannot be damaged upon hitting the ground. On this particular day, the rainclouds above had brought the answer to me.

P.134. EPHEMERA

An anchor—which of course, you throw out of your boat only when it's needed, and bring back when you no longer require it. It occurs to me now that a fishing net would also fit the brief, as that too only becomes most useful when it is cast away from its owner.

P.137. THE SPHINX

Thursday. Taking "yesterday" to mean the day before the day on which the Sphinx is speaking, then "if yesterday were tomorrow" leads you to the day before this. As we know that day would be Tuesday, then the day must be two days after Tuesday, i.e. Thursday.

Another interpretation of the puzzle could be that the answer is Sunday, if you instead take "if yesterday were tomorrow" to refer to the hypothetical day in question. In this case then "yesterday" refers to the day before Tuesday, which is Monday, so the answer would then be the day when Monday is tomorrow: Sunday.

P.138. THE WRITING ON THE WALL

A secret, which ceases to exist the moment it is shared.

P.140. LOST IN TRANSLATION

The doctor must have been a woman, and so been the deceased man's sister. I was, I confess, rather embarrassed at my oversight, and decided it was best that I should focus on my own notation for a while, instead of the work of others.

P.142. THE COUNTESS'S TRICK

Fifty-six years old. Taking away the three days the countess mentioned leaves only four days in each of her "weeks", suggesting that her figure of thirty-two is four-sevenths of her real age. Thirty-two divided by four and then multiplied by seven (the number of days in a regular week) gives her real age, fifty-six.

P.143. SACRED BIRDS

It is true. For there to be more ibises than feathers on any single ibis, there would have to be at least one ibis which had no feathers. Imagine a hypothetical world where there are ten ibises in total, the first with one feather, the second with two feathers, the third with three feathers and so on, with the ninth bird having nine feathers (and yes, I am aware this is a somewhat ridiculous thought experiment, but bear with me). As the statement says there are more ibises in the world than feathers on a single ibis, the tenth ibis *cannot* have ten or more feathers—and since it also cannot have zero feathers (as no ibises are featherless), then it must have from one to nine feathers. This in turn would mean that there will be at least two ibises with the same number of feathers, and so the statement is true.

P.144. THE UNENDING QUEST

The horizon, which can never be reached, whatever distance you travel towards it. It was a rather depressing thought, I suppose, although one's quest for the horizon might take one on some wonderful travels.

P.146. SEEING IS BELIEVING

A school, or perhaps a library—where one might enter it without knowledge and be said to be blind, and leave it having learned a little (or a lot), thus being able to "see". It's a rather poetic interpretation, I suppose, but I found myself quite fond of this scholarly riddle. A religious building, such as a church, might also be considered to have a similar effect.

P.148. A DIVIDED KINGDOM

He got one child to divide the land into two parts, then got the other child to choose which part they wanted.

P.149. ANCIENT NUMBERS

6,210,001,000

P.150. A CHAGRIN

Nothing. Once I had seen the contents, or rather the lack thereof, I could not help but suffer a wry smile—whoever had sealed this box and clued us to its "contents" in this way was clearly something of a wag.

P.152. CONTENTS

Candles—which, as an aside, might well have been invented by the ancient Egyptians. A thin candle burns quickly, and a thick one slowly; a tall candle is "young" as it cannot have been used for long, and a short one must therefore be "old".

P.154. LIFE AND DEATH

A fire—which needs fuel to grow, but will be extinguished by water.

P.155. TRANSLITERATION

The word "erroneously"—which will, of course, always be spelled like this: "erroneously".

P.156. THE PRINCESS'S TALE

The boy could have looked at the princess's reflection—a reflection being often seen in water but not being able to get wet. It occurs to me that the princess could have more explicitly suggested that he find a mirror, to give the poor boy a helping hand.

P.158. THE TROUBLE WITH TWO

They could have been two in a set of triplets—or quadruplets, or indeed part of any multiple birth with more than two children. In that way, they could be born on the same day of the same year to the same mother, but still not be twins.

P.159. FLIGHT OF FANCY
An arrow—which has feathers and flies through the air, but has no wings to speak of. I wonder that it took me so long to find the answer, with the bow and arrow being as ubiquitous as they were in ancient Egypt!

P.160. THE BLOCKS
There were forty-four blocks left in the stack—and indeed it took forty-four hours to move them all. It was a long and arduous task; fortunately I was only charged with the calculation, and not the manual effort!

P.162. A BREAKTHROUGH
An egg—which must be broken open before it can be used, and which I was partial to enjoying during breakfast of a morning.

P.163. SEE AND BE SEEN
The pupils in your eyes, which grow smaller when there is more light.

P.164. APPRENTICES
Cross your arms, as you would if you were waiting rather impatiently for someone to get to the end of a tedious story. Next, pick up one end of the string in each hand and, as you uncross your arms, the string will be tied in a simple knot. Or at least, that's what his mentor told me later; apparently the boy had tried this trick on a few other excavators.

P.166. THE TOUR
A postage stamp—which can travel across the world without ever leaving the corner of the envelope that it is stuck to.

P.167. A WHOLE NEW PROBLEM
A hole, which gets bigger the more that you take away from it. In our line of work, digging hole after hole, it seemed rather obvious to me. But to anyone else, perhaps, it is somewhat more of a riddle.

P.168. ORDERLY
The prince was buried first, in the mid-sized chamber. The queen was buried second, in the smallest chamber, and the king was buried last, in the largest.

P.170. PAPYRUS AND PAILS
The water-drawer should fill the 8-unit pail to the top, and then use it to fill the 5-unit pail, leaving exactly 3 units in the larger pail. They should empty then the 5-unit pail into the river and pour the 3 units from the 8-unit pail to the 5-unit pail. This leaves exactly 2 units of empty space in the 5-unit pail. Finally, the water-drawer should fill the 8-unit pail to the brim once more and then use it to fill the 5-unit pail to the brim. This would involve pouring out exactly 2 units—leaving exactly 6 units in the 8-unit pail.

P.172. THE HIEROGLYPHIC PYRAMID
The final line would have read:
I I III I II II I I III
The sequence is written in hieroglyphs, where I = 1, II = 2 and III = 3.
When replaced with modern numerals, the following emerges:

```
            3
          1 3
        1 1 1 3
        3 1 1 3
      1 3 2 1 1 3
```

The code can be explained by reading the numbers in each line aloud, with each subsequent line stating out loud the counts of numbers which appear in the line immediately preceding. To whit, in the first line there is but a single '3'—and so the second line reads '1 3', since there is indeed 'one 3'.

Then, in the following line, there is one '1' and one '3'—and thus the next step down is scratched as '1 1 1 3'. This pattern then carries on down the pyramid.

The final line of the puzzle, then, would be written out as '1x1 1x3 1x2 2x1 1x3'—or in hieroglyphs as "I I I III I II II I I III".

P.174. ONE MAN'S TREASURE...
A long-sleeved shirt—which has a neck and arms, but no head and hands. How this modern shirt came to be buried in the sand here is a mystery, but not of the kind I should like to waste my time solving.

P.175. INSIDE AND OUTSIDE
Corn (or maize), where the outer leaves are first peeled, and the kernels within are cooked. In turn, those kernels (which are now the outside of the cob) are removed, and the inner core thrown away.

P.176. A WORTHY WINNER
Neither sibling won the race. If the older brother was in second place as he approached the line, then he must have moved to third place when his younger sister overtook him—and someone else entirely was the race winner.

P.178. BRICK BY BRICK
Just one—indeed only one will ever be needed to *complete* any

building. One might be inclined to presume, on a pyramid, that it will always be the top one.

P.180. MODERN CHARIOTS
To let the air out of the tyres. Not something the ancient chariot-drivers would have been able to do, of course! With the air thus removed, the top of the automobile would drop and be no longer wedged beneath the lintel.

P.181. A DISAPPOINTING DISCOVERY
A hole. Whatever the sack had once contained—grains, or glass beads or some such—had long since spilled out.

P.182. THE CREATURE
The *shadow* of a cat, against his tent. Indeed, it would have been exactly the size and shape of a cat, but left no marks inside the tent, and been quite intangible. Most likely it was created in the shadow cast by someone's torch—quite ephemeral, but hardly a fearsome creature at all.

P.184. THE FAST
The man could eat and drink at night, and not during any day.

P.185. OF THE REIGNS OF KINGS
The years are in years B.C., not A.D., and so they are effectively -1344 and -1325. Therefore 19 years after 1344 B.C. is indeed 1325 B.C.

P.186. THE WATER CLOCK
I had left the clock out in the hot sun, and all of the water had evaporated. Needless to say, I was not overly enthused to show the results to my patron, whom I had otherwise hoped would consider me to be a sensible sort of apprentice.

P.188. BACK TO RECTANGLE ONE

There are 303 squares and rectangles. We never did reach a conclusion as to how many of the tiles were preserved in their original size but we were rather tired from all the counting, by that stage.

P.190. SOCIAL NICETIES

None at all. Using myself as an example, if I had met anyone who had journeyed to more places than me, then they would nonetheless have been unable to shake my hand, since they could only shake hands with those who had journeyed to more places than themselves. Therefore nobody could shake anybody's hand at all. Fortunately this flaw was soon discovered and the exercise abandoned, and I was free to return to the room.

P.191. WEEP AND WORSHIP

An onion. When it is cut and peeled, onion famously has a lachrymose effect on those nearby. The onion—humble as it may seem to the horticulturalist—was revered by the ancient Egyptians; the layers within were seen as a symbol of everlasting life.

P.192. TROUBLE BREWING

The sisters should pour two of the half-filled vessels into one empty vessel. Then there would be six full vessels, three half-full vessels, and six empty vessels. Each sister could then take two each of the full and empty vessels, and a half-full one.

P.194. THE AMULETS

One way to do it is shown opposite—crucially, the original three points of the triangle (darkest shaded circles) must

move to become the three new points (middle shaded), while the others (lightest shaded) retain their position. Needless to say, I instructed my colleague to take a step back while I continued to record the remaining contents of the tomb.

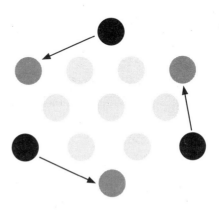

P.196. RISING WATER

Never, since the bait wouldn't enter the water at all. Anything attached to the boat would rise with the boat as the water levels rose—so the line would never be any closer to the water. I suppose he might have been lucky if there were some sort of flying or leaping fish in the river, but 2 feet would be quite a jump.

P.197. NATURAL PHENOMENON

A hailstone. Being made of pure water, it could never get any wetter.

P.198. THE PLOUGH

None at all. There were no oxen footsteps to count—when an ox ploughs, it turns the soil behind it, meaning that there would be no evidence of their hooves left to reckon with. It was a rather cruel trick, I think, and even crueller that the boy's humiliation should be painted on a wall for eternity.

P.200. LOOTED LOOT

I could have moved one disc from any corner and placed it on top of the disc in its diagonally opposite corner. In that way there would be two straight rows with three discs in each, one horizontal and one vertical. Needless to say, I didn't waste time explaining this to the challenger.

P.202. AN URN-EST PROBLEM

The mirrored surfaces should be placed as follows:

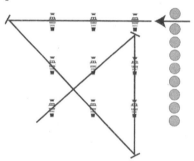

P.204. THE LONGEST RIVER

It was, of course, still the Nile, whose length and course remained stoically unaltered by the mere fact of its discovery.

P.205. PAINTED PHARAOHS

The ancient Egyptians didn't have our modern technology, so they simply never painted pharaohs with photographic cameras. Therefore, It was not possible to record paintings of such scenes— as they did not exist!

P.206. SNAKING SOLUTION

The snake should be threaded as follows:

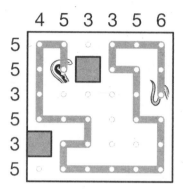

P.208. HEAVEN AND EARTH

An earthworm. The pharaoh Cleopatra apparently so revered this limbless creature that she created laws to make sure they weren't removed from the lands they helped to fertilize. Modern gardeners would no doubt agree— although probably not on their divine nature.